In the Kitchen with Bob

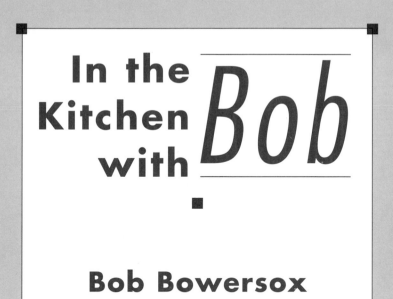

In the Kitchen with Bob

Bob Bowersox

Hearst Books
New York

Library of Congress Cataloging-in-Publication Data

Bowersox, Bob.
    In the kitchen with Bob / Bob Bowersox.
       p.   cm.
    ISBN 0-688-13797-0
    1. Cookery.   I. Title.
    TX714.B644   1994
    641.5—dc20   94-11426
                               CIP

Printed in the United States of America

First Edition

2 3 4 5 6 7 8 9 10

BOOK DESIGN BY RICHARD ORIOLO

*This book is dedicated to
my wife and partner, Toni, and
to our daughter, Taylor Tracey,
the best recipe we've ever
come up with*

Acknowledgments

I've always believed that books bearing the name of a single author were the result of that writer's solitary effort. I have had to alter that belief. There are a remarkable number of people connected to the evolution of this work. Some are aware of their involvement; others I've never met, but they've been involved nonetheless. I owe all a debt of gratitude.

First and foremost, I wish to thank the viewers of QVC for their support and encouragement of my efforts, both on the air and on the page. Special thanks to Doug Briggs, President of QVC-Electronic Retailing, for his immediate enthusiasm for the project, and to the planning group who have made *In the Kitchen with Bob* possible: buyers Sandy Conrad and Kathy Harper and programmers Karen Leever, Rich Maurer, and Michelle Okuniewski. Thanks also to the producers and control room staff, and to every product coordinator who has ever picked up a knife to help with the prep, especially Sue Roberts and Bill Hambrook, who have never let me down. Thanks also to Jack

Comstock, Sue Schick, Mark Bozek, Len Czabator, Fred Siegel, Carla Jordan, and their respective staffs at QVC.

Thanks to Bill Adler for seeing the possibilities and opening the doors, and to Megan Newman for immediate friendship and wise guidance. And thanks to Toni, Taylor, and Stephanie for allowing me to disappear upstairs every night.

And finally, a very special thank you to you who paved the way, and have educated and entertained me with your expertise and wit for so long: Julia, Jacques, Jeff, Graham, Yan, Art, Paul, and a score of others. You showed me that the love of cooking can take you anywhere.

Contents

Introduction

■

I vividly remember the first time I cooked something. It was a warm, early summer evening in Denver, Colorado. I was eight or nine years old, a budding young Cub Scout facing the daunting reality of my first overnight camping trip. Though I was looking forward to the exhilaration of being free from parental supervision for the first time in my life, I was conversely facing the cold reality that dinner wasn't just going to appear in front of me, as it had magically every night without fail. I realized that if my stomach was to be warm and full, I was going to have to do the warming and filling.

I was terrified. Bears, snakes, wolves—no problem for a tough scout. Cooking a burger? My God!

My father, obviously sympatico, knew just what to do. He put his arm around my shoulders and led me to the kitchen, where he handed me a plate, some raw burger, two pieces of bread, a frying pan, a knife, a fork, a spatula, and some matches. Calmed and sensing salvation at hand, I followed him into the backyard. He had me gather some twigs and small branches, and pile them loosely in the center of a circle of bricks he'd arranged at the edge of a garden.

"Now cook yourself dinner," he said, smiling and winking at me. Then he turned, went back into the house, and closed the door.

To this day I'm so very thankful it was my mother who taught me how to swim.

But in all fairness, I owe my father a great deal, for he taught me the greatest lesson I could have learned about cooking: it's not nearly as mysterious or complicated as one might imagine it to be. I cooked that hamburger, and I remember it being the best burger I'd ever tasted. I also remember being somewhat surprised at how simple it had been to make what, to me, was a great meal. It hadn't required any special technologies or skills; just the curiosity to see if I could do it, and the willingness to try. Being hungry didn't hurt, either.

I've carried that lesson with me ever since, through my career as a restaurateur, and into my current position as chef and host of *In the Kitchen with Bob* on the QVC Network. Cooking stylish dishes well is *not* a complicated undertaking. Nor does it require a great deal of time. All you really need is a sense of adventure and some enthusiasm. And anyone who likes to eat will have those ingredients in abundance.

You see that adventure and enthusiasm on *In the Kitchen with Bob* every week. I truly love to cook and to experiment with cooking, and it's my hope that I impart how easy it is to cook well without the process being overly involved or precise or exasperating. Since any one product presentation on QVC only lasts eight to ten minutes, I also enjoy the challenge of completing a stylish and enticing dish in a short time.

Dealing on a weekly basis with the twin necessities of simplicity and efficiency have led to the writing of this cookbook. Over the last three years I've created hundreds of recipes that are quick and easy to prepare, delicious, and colorful to serve. And because of the realities of how I must cook, I've developed a number of little tricks that have helped me adapt hundreds of other recipes to my needs—recipes that would normally take up to an hour to prepare and can now be done in minutes.

This book is the response to the thousands of weekly requests I receive to share those recipes and shortcuts in a more permanent way. It includes the most requested recipes I've prepared since *In the Kitchen with Bob* premiered three years ago, and a number of new ones that will be prepared on shows planned through the coming year. When I have adapted a recipe from another cookbook, chef, or writer, I have identified the source so you might delve further into that cook's approaches or prepare the recipe in its long form when you have the time and inclination to do so. Regardless of origin, the choices were made to render meals or dishes a few notches above standard "quick-cooking" fare, without sacrificing simplicity or efficiency in preparation.

The cooking of most of the dishes can be completed in under ten minutes. Some of them, like the soups, stews, or casseroles, will, of course, require simmering or baking for an hour or so. But you should have everything in the pot in just a few minutes, and you can let the stove or oven do the rest of the work for you.

I'll let you get to it. So, with a wink and a smile, I'm going to go back into the house. Enjoy.

Soups, Stews, and Chilis

To make good soup, the pot must only ''smile'' [simmer], not ''laugh outloud'' [boil].

—Old French Proverb

I have always been in love with soups. I can't remember a time when I wouldn't choose a soup over a sandwich for lunch, and my first question at any restaurant is about the soups.

I think what intrigues me so much are the dynamics soups can have. They can be so subtle that you're almost not aware of the perfect balance in them, like the Herbed Celery Soup or Chilled Melon Soup included here. But they can also be made to trumpet their heartiness, as in the Hamilton Gazpacho or Bowersox Onion Soup. Some soups, like the authentic German Kartoffelsuppe, Japanese Yosenabe, or traditional French Fish Pot-au-Feu, are indeed meals in themselves, and should be considered for those afternoons or nights when such a soup is all that is needed.

Stews and chilis are close cousins of soups, and I've included a number of viewer favorites here. You can choose from popular traditionals like Classic Irish Stew, Bouillabaisse, or Bayou Gumbo, or strike out onto some interesting ground with Brazil's exotic Vatapa, Lyndon

Baines Johnson's personally created Pedernales River Chili, or the marvelous Jambalaya Louis Armstrong, created by the famous jazz trumpeter and shared with me by a QVC viewer. These may take a little longer to simmer to perfection, but most of the ingredients will be in the pot in a few minutes, leaving you free to relax and enjoy family, friends, or guests.

Herbed Celery Soup

Makes 4 servings

The recipe for celery soup is said to have originated in an early Indiana settlement, circa 1814, where it was the first meal served to travelers who arrived at the settlement. Journalist Bernard Clayton, Jr., found the recipe in an obscure cookbook from that era and translated it into the present day. I have slightly adapted his version here. The clean, crisp, simple taste of celery is balanced with a mix of distinctive herbs. It's a terrifically refreshing soup for the high heat of summer or the chill of winter.

2 tablespoons butter or margarine
2 cups finely chopped celery
1 teaspoon chopped dried chives
¾ teaspoon chopped dried tarragon
¼ teaspoon chopped dried chervil
4 cups chicken stock
⅛ teaspoon sugar
Salt and pepper to taste
4 slices French bread
Nutmeg (as garnish)

1 Melt the butter in a medium saucepan and add the celery, chives, tarragon, and chervil. Cover and cook for 5 minutes or until celery has softened.

2 Add the chicken stock, sugar, and any salt and pepper you desire. Simmer over low heat for about 20 minutes.

3 Just before serving, toast the bread, preferably under a broiler. Place a piece of bread in each soup bowl, and ladle the soup over the bread. Garnish with a pinch of ground nutmeg.

Read Before Beginning

Read through the entire recipe and preparation instructions before beginning any preparation or cooking. Set the procedures loosely in your mind, and familiarize yourself with any timings. It will definitely save you time in the execution of the recipe.

Fish and Spinach Soup

Simple, different, down-to-earth, nutritious, low-calorie, only minutes to prepare. I fell in love with it instantly.

FOR THE MARINADE
1 teaspoon dry white wine
¼ teaspoon salt
1 teaspoon cornstarch

6 cups chicken stock
1 to 2 slices fresh ginger, ⅛ inch thick
¼ pound white fish fillets, cut into 1 × 2 × ¼-inch slices
½ pound spinach, cleaned and washed, long stems removed
½ teaspoon salt
¼ teaspoon oriental sesame oil (use the hot version for a little zing)
White pepper to taste

1 Prepare the marinade and marinate the fish for 30 minutes before preparing the soup.

2 In a large stockpot or Dutch oven, bring the chicken stock and the ginger to a boil over high heat.

3 Add all the other ingredients, and reduce the heat to medium-low. Cook only until spinach is wilted, a few minutes. Fish will be done by then. Serve hot.

Unbelievably Good Garlic Soup

Makes 2 servings

My father, Don Bowersox, worked on this recipe for about eight years. At least once a month he'd have me over for a "garlic orgy," featuring the soup, Caesar salad, and garlic bread. When he'd finally perfected the recipe, Mom put a halt to the orgies, saying that it took her two weeks to get the smell of garlic out of the house. But the recipes live on. If you like garlic as much as we Bowersoxes, this soup is for you.

2 medium onions, chopped
1 head garlic (that's the *entire* head, not just 1 clove!), cloves separated and peeled
3 tablespoons olive oil
1 cup chicken stock
1 cup cream or half-and-half
Day-old French bread, cut into bits
2 teaspoons paprika
¼ teaspoon ground cumin
Salt and pepper to taste
Chopped fresh parsley (as garnish)

1 In a large skillet, over medium heat, sauté the onions and garlic in the olive oil until the onions are translucent, about 5 minutes.

2 Transfer the sautéed mixture to a blender or food processor and blend until smooth. Add the chicken stock and continue to blend; then add the cream and blend well. If you have an adjustable-speed processor, you might find the mixture staying smoother on a slower blending speed, you don't want to froth the cream.

3 Add small bits of the French bread slowly, so that the soup begins to thicken up as the bread is incorporated into the liquid. The amount of bread you add is going to determine the thickness of your soup. If you want a thick, almost stewlike consistency, add more bread. If you want a thinner soup, add less.

4 Once you have the texture you want, transfer the mixture to a saucepan over medium heat. Add the paprika and cumin, and salt and pepper to taste. Simmer for 5 to 8 minutes. Sprinkle with parsley and serve hot.

Quick Consommé

A classic and classy beginning to any multicourse meal. I've always loved consommé, and have evolved this recipe over the years by combining features of many others.

5 cups beef bone stock or beef broth
4 ounces lean boneless beef, finely chopped
2 egg whites
5 black peppercorns
½ teaspoon salt
¼ to ⅓ cup dry sherry
1 green onion (dark green tops only), cut into slivers 3 inches long (as garnish)
1 3-inch stick of carrot, cut into slivers (as garnish)

1 Place the stock or broth in a large saucepan and heat it slowly until nearly boiling. Add the beef, egg whites, peppercorns, and salt. Bring to a vigorous boil, stirring frequently with a wire whisk. Reduce heat and simmer for 1 hour.

2 Strain the liquid through cheesecloth or an exceptionally fine wire-mesh strainer.

3 Add the sherry and simmer another 3 to 5 minutes.

4 Serve hot, with a few slivers of green onion and carrot floating on top.

Food Processors

One of the greatest timesavers we have is the food processor. In my kitchen, I actually have three: a full-size, a smaller 3-cup version, and a minichopper/grinder. For onions, garlic, celery, bread crumbs, spices—anything I need to chop, dice, or mince quickly—they are unequaled. If you can equip yourself with only one, I suggest the minichopper/grinder; it will save you enormous time while doing a superior job.

Quick Bermuda
Fish Chowder

Makes 4 servings

2 pounds fresh fish fillets
(cod, scrod, haddock,
grouper, snapper, or a
mix of them), with-
out skin
½ teaspoon salt
½ teaspoon dried thyme,
or 1 tablespoon fresh
1 bay leaf
3 to 4 whole cloves
3 to 4 black peppercorns
¼ pound salt pork, diced
2 medium onions,
chopped
6 stalks celery, chopped
1 medium green bell
pepper, seeded and
chopped
3 medium tomatoes,
seeded and chopped
1 10¾-ounce can
concentrated beef
consommé
¼ 28-ounce bottle catsup
6 parsley sprigs, minced
3 tablespoons
Worcestershire sauce
⅛ teaspoon curry
powder
2 tablespoons flour
1 teaspoon gravy
browning
1 tablespoon lemon juice
Dark rum (optional)
Outerbridge's Original
Sherry Peppers Sauce
(or sherry, if you're
unlucky enough not to
have any
Outerbridge's—also
optional)

Bermuda may be my favorite place on earth. I love the sweet, spicy scent of the air, the phenomenal blue color of the waters surrounding the coral beaches, the warmness of the sun and the people—and the fish chowder. There probably are as many recipes for Bermuda Fish Chowder as there are cooks on Bermuda, each one different, all lovely. This one is a distillation of several recipes I've enjoyed.

1 Place the fish in a large stockpot, and add water to cover. Also add the salt, thyme, bay leaf, cloves, and peppercorns. Bring to a boil, then reduce heat and simmer for about 1 hour. Remove any fish bones, and flake the fish fillets into shreds.

2 In a separate large skillet or saucepan, fry the salt pork with the onions, celery, and green pepper. When the pork is cooked through and the vegetables are wilting, in about 5 minutes, add the tomatoes, consommé, catsup, parsley, Worcestershire sauce, and curry powder. Simmer another 8 to 10 minutes to blend the flavors, then add this to the fish mixture in the stockpot.

3 Mix the flour with about 2 tablespoons of the liquid from the stockpot until blended, then add to the stockpot. This should help thicken the soup a bit. Also add the gravy browning to darken the soup's color. Simmer another 15 minutes.

4 Just before serving add the lemon juice. Have a cruet of rum and the Outerbridge's sauce or sherry on the table to add as desired.

Kartoffelsuppe
German Potato Soup

Makes about 4 servings

I must thank Barbara Prendergast, one of the loan officers at my bank, for this recipe. Barbara is from Munich, and when I mentioned how much I enjoyed *Kartoffelsuppe* but could find no authentic recipe for it, she immediately offered this, her family's recipe. It is marvelous, and has the authentic taste I'd been trying to achieve.

½ pound lean bacon
1 medium onion, diced
2 medium leeks, trimmed of roots and dark tops, diced
2 celery stalks, julienned
3 medium carrots, julienned
¼ cup finely chopped fresh parsley
6 cups beef stock
2 pounds potatoes, diced (about ¼- to ⅜-inch cubes)
1 bay leaf
10 black peppercorns
3 juniper berries (optional)
1 teaspoon caraway seeds
½ teaspoon ground nutmeg
½ teaspoon dried marjoram (optional)
Salt and pepper to taste
½ cup sour cream (optional)
Fresh parsley sprigs (garnish)

1 Cut the bacon into 1-inch squares and place in a large saucepan or Dutch oven. Slowly fry it over medium heat. When it is just short of being crisp, remove the bacon, draining and reserving it.

2 Add the onion, leeks, celery, carrots, and parsley and cook until the onion wilts. Add the beef stock and potatoes; raise heat to high and bring to a boil. Add the bay leaf, peppercorns, juniper berries, caraway seeds, and nutmeg. Boil for 20 to 25 minutes or until the potatoes are soft when pierced with a fork. Add the reserved bacon pieces.

3 At this point, you can go one of two ways: You can serve the soup as a clear soup, sprinkling it with a little marjoram, salt, and pepper; or remove the potatoes with a slotted spoon, placing them in a large bowl. Mash them, and add ½ cup sour cream and blend thoroughly. Then stir potatoes back into the soup. This makes a creamier style Kartoffelsuppe.

4 In both cases, remove bay leaf and add a sprig or two of parsley on top of the soup before serving.

Prep All Recipe Items Before You Begin Cooking

My efficiency in preparing the dishes on *In the Kitchen with Bob* is due to primarily one thing: the preparation we do before we go on air. We prep every item we'll be using. You benefit in several ways by doing this:

- It's easier to do one type of work all at once, using the same tools.
- You're not splitting your attention—that is, trying to cut a vegetable and watch a skillet at the same time.
- You can arrange all the ingredients on your workspace in the order in which they'll be used.
- Your cooking will be more calm and controlled; you'll be able to enjoy yourself more.

Hamilton Gazpacho

This is another soup I learned to love in Bermuda (of all places). I coaxed the recipe from the chef at a restaurant on Front Street in Hamilton, and have played with it for a couple of years since. I've come to like it spicy, but you can tone it down by taking it easy with the Tabasco and cutting the garlic a bit. It's a great summer soup that's best if served chilled right from the refrigerator.

1 Coarsely chop about ¼ cup each of the green pepper, onion, and cucumber. Set aside.

1 medium to large green bell pepper, seeded and quartered
1 large onion, quartered
1 medium cucumber, peeled and cubed
3 medium, ripe tomatoes, seeded, peeled, and quartered
4 garlic cloves
1 2-ounce jar pimientos
3 cups tomato juice
⅓ cup red wine vinegar
¼ cup extra-virgin olive oil
⅔ cup chicken stock
6 to 8 large dashes of Tabasco sauce (less, if you don't want it all that hot)
Salt and pepper to taste
Garlic croutons (as garnish in soup)

2 In a large blender or food processor, place the tomatoes, remaining green pepper, onion, and cucumber, the garlic, and the pimientos and blend thoroughly. Pour into a large bowl and add the tomato juice, vinegar, oil, stock, Tabasco, and salt and pepper. Stir thoroughly with a wire whisk.

3 Add the reserved chopped pepper, onion, and cucumber, stirring again. Cover and refrigerate for several hours or until well chilled. Stir up the chopped vegetables before ladling into bowls, and drop in a few croutons before serving.

Bowersox Onion Soup

My father thought that most onion soups were watery and had no gusto (that wasn't his exact word, but it will suffice). And as usual, he hammered away at it until he had a recipe he thought was what onion soup should be. I agree. This is an onion lover's soup—rich and dark, tangy and spirited. They don't make them like this in restaurants. The secret is in taking the time to caramelize the onions.

8 medium to large onions
4 tablespoons butter or
   margarine
2 10¾-ounce cans
   concentrated beef
   consommé
2 cans water
½ teaspoon salt
½ teaspoon
   Worcestershire sauce
½ loaf French bread, cut
   into 2-inch-thick rounds
Mozzarella or Provolone
   cheese, thinly sliced
Grated Parmesan cheese

1 Cut the onions in ⅜-inch slices, then cut the slices in half.

2 In a 4-quart stockpot or Dutch oven, sauté the onions in the butter. Do this *very slowly*, over a medium heat until deep, dark brown, with a thickened, almost caramelized texture without being burned. This should take a minimum of 20 minutes.

3 Add the consommé, water, salt, and Worcestershire sauce and simmer until hot. Preheat the broiler.

4 Place 1 piece of the French bread in individual ramkins or high-sided, broiler-safe bowls. Ladle the soup over the bread until it is covered and the soup is near the top of the ramkins or bowls. Cover the ramkins or bowls with the mozzarella cheese, and place under broiler until the cheese is melted and beginning to brown on top. Serve with grated cheese.

Fish Pot-au-Feu

*P*ot-au-Feu literally means "pot on the fire," and its preparation is usually considered an all-day affair. Pot-au-Feu can be made with beef, fowl, or fish plus any number of vegetables—it usually depends on what the French workman brings home the day the soup is made. This recipe is a distillation of many that I've come across, but designed to be lighter than most and make use of one of my favorite herbs, tarragon.

5 cups fish stock (see following recipe) or full-strength chicken stock

1 cup dry white wine

1½ tablespoons chopped fresh tarragon leaves, or ¾ teaspoon chopped dried

4 small red-skinned potatoes

4 medium carrots, peeled and cut into 2-inch lengths

4 small leeks, roots, dark green tops, and torn outer leaves trimmed

1 medium Bermuda onion, cut into ¼-inch slices

1½ pounds white fish fillets (cod, scrod, haddock, red snapper, or mahimahi), without skin

Salt and pepper to taste

1 In a Dutch oven or large stockpot over high heat, combine the stock, wine, and tarragon. Let it come to a boil, then add the potatoes and carrots. When the pot comes to a boil again, reduce the heat just enough to maintain a vigorous simmer. Hold that simmer for about 10 minutes.

2 Split the leeks lengthwise and rinse them well—they usually have a great deal of sand in them. Place them in a frying pan wide enough to hold their length with about ¼ inch of water. Cover and steam gently until the leeks are tender enough to pierce with a fork but not dull and mushy, about 8 to 10 minutes.

3 Meanwhile, wash and trim the fish, and cut into 4 equal portions. Add to the Dutch oven. Add the onion, cover and simmer until the fish is poached through and is beginning to flake when touched with a fork. Time it so that the vegetables will also be tender when stuck with a fork. (Plan on the fish taking only about 5 minutes to poach, so when the vegetables are just about right, add the fish.)

4 With a slotted spoon, gently lift the fish fillets from the pot and place one piece in the center of each individual soup bowl. (It's best if the bowls are the wide, shallow type.) Evenly divide the vegetables among the bowls and ladle the broth over all. Serve with salt and pepper for individual tastes.

A Good, Basic Fish Stock

Certain fish don't make good stock. It is best to use the heads and carcasses of fish such as haddock, cod, red snapper, grouper, or bass. Stay away from sole, flounder, and halibut.

3 tablespoons butter or margarine
½ cup chopped shallots
¼ cup chopped carrot
½ cup chopped celery
6 white peppercorns
3 whole cloves
½ cup dry white wine
½ cup chopped fresh parsley
1 bay leaf
2 sprigs fresh thyme
3 cups cold water
1 ½ pounds washed fish bones, heads, and trimmings (do not use entrails, gills, or skin)
3 tablespoons lemon juice

1 Melt the butter or margarine in a large stockpot, and add the shallots, carrot, and celery. Bring to a boil, then reduce heat to produce a calm simmer. Add the peppercorns, cloves, wine, parsley, bay leaf, thyme, and water.

2 Thoroughly rinse the fish and add to the stockpot. Bring to a boil, skimming off any scum or fat that comes to the surface. Reduce the heat, cover, and simmer for 45 minutes.

3 Strain and discard all solids. The stock is now ready to use. It can be kept in the refrigerator for up to 3 days, and frozen for up to 3 months.

Chilled Melon Soup

Fragrant and rich in flavor, this is a great warm-weather soup. I acquired a taste for it on my honeymoon at Caneel Bay, on St. John's, in the Virgin Islands. The chef served it as the opening course every night. It is best when made with cantaloupe or honeydew at the peak of ripeness. This is one of the best versions I've come across, found in Bernard Clayton, Jr.'s *Soups and Stews.*

2 medium cantaloupes or honeydews
2 cups apricot nectar
1 cup water
2 tablespoons honey
1 tablespoon lemon juice
⅛ teaspoon salt

SPICE PACKET
1 cinnamon stick
3 whole allspice
1 whole clove
1½-inch slice fresh ginger

1 cup light cream, chilled
1 tablespoon apricot or peach brandy (optional)
Fresh mint leaves (as garnish)

1 Cut the rind from the fruit, seed it, and slice it into 1-inch chunks. Place in a saucepan with the apricot nectar, water, honey, lemon juice, and salt. Stir together well and add the spice packet (best if placed in a cheesecloth bag or teaball). Bring to a boil, then reduce heat so liquids and fruit simmer gently until the fruit is soft, about 10 minutes.

2 Remove from heat and allow to cool slightly. Remove the spice packet, and put fruit mixture in a large blender or food processor. Puree thoroughly, then refrigerate until chilled.

3 Just before serving, stir chilled cream into the soup and add the optional brandy. Garnish with mint leaves and serve immediately.

Make a Double Batch

Whenever possible, make a double batch of your favorite soup. Use one half the night you prepare it, and freeze the other half for an easy, quickly prepared meal some other night.

Southwest Corn Soup

Makes 6 servings

Is there anything as wonderfully sweet as Silver Queen corn just off the stalk in August? I count the days every summer until the harvest is ready from the New Jersey fields. I came across this recipe in Sunset's *Southwest Cook Book,* and thought how great it might be with East Coast Silver Queen. I wasn't disappointed. It's delicious with any corn, but irresistible with Silver Queen.

4 tablespoons butter or margarine

3½ cups Silver Queen corn kernels, cut from just-picked cobs

1 garlic clove, minced

1 cup chicken stock

2 cups milk

1 teaspoon dried oregano

1 4-ounce can diced green chilies

1 cup shredded Monterey Jack cheese

Salt to taste

Fresh cilantro or oregano sprigs (as garnish)

1 Melt the butter in a Dutch oven over medium heat. Add the corn and garlic, and cook, stirring frequently, until the corn is hot, about 2 minutes. Remove from heat.

2 Place 2 cups of the hot corn in a blender or food processor with the stock and puree. Return the puree to the Dutch oven.

3 Stir in the milk, oregano, and chilies. Bring to a boil, stirring. Remove from heat and stir in the cheese. Season with salt. Serve with a sprig of cilantro or oregano placed on top of the soup in the bowls.

Salsa Fish Soup

Makes 4 servings

6 cups chicken stock
⅔ cup quick-cooking rice
2 cups corn kernels (from the cob or frozen)
1 pound skinless mild-flavored fish fillets (haddock, cod, or halibut)
1½ cups hot, chunk-style salsa (or mild, if you'd prefer)
Lime wedges

I'm not sure how this recipe came to be in my files. Perhaps it was a viewer who knew my likes, or something I ended up with after a recipe-trading and wine-tasting evening with my brother. However the good fortune came to me, this soup combines two of my loves—salsa and fish—and is easy to make as well. A perfect combination.

1 In a 5- or 6-quart stockpot, combine the stock and the rice, and bring to a boil over high heat. Reduce the heat and cover, simmering until the rice is tender, about 5 minutes.

2 Add the corn, fish, and salsa. Cover and simmer until the fish is opaque and flakes when touched with a fork. Ladle into bowls carefully, so as not to break fish up too much. Serve with lime wedges to squeeze into soup.

Crab Chowder

Makes 12 servings

A nice twist on cool-weather soups, this is a great chowder for shellfish lovers. And unlike most chowders, it's low in total fat. Try this for the next church banquet, when you have little time to come up with a lot of something appetizing. It's surprisingly quick and easy to prepare. One note: it is traditional that all ingredients in a chowder are about the same size, so cut and chop them accordingly.

2 tablespoons vege-
table oil
2 small onions, finely
chopped
1 pound fresh
mushrooms, thinly
sliced
1 teaspoon dried thyme
4 cups coarsely chopped
broccoli flowerettes
1 cup chopped green bell
pepper
1 cup chopped red bell
pepper
4 cups chicken stock
4 cups low-fat milk
2 16-ounce cans
cream-style corn
12 ounces crabmeat,
picked clean
6 cups cooked long-grain
white rice
Salt and pepper

1 Heat the oil in a large stockpot. Add the onions, mushrooms, and thyme, and cook, stirring, until the vegetables begin to brown. Add the broccoli and peppers, and continue to cook until the broccoli begins to turn bright green, about 4 minutes.

2 Stir in the stock, milk, and corn, and cook until cooked through, but do not boil. Stir in the crabmeat and rice, and again cook until heated through.

3 Season to taste with salt and pepper, and serve hot.

Yosenabe

I've been studying the Japanese language for about a year now, and have been drawn into the cuisine through my studies. One of my favorite parts of Japanese cooking is the soups. Clear and flavorful, each recipe seems to have its own surprises. Yosenabe is one of the best. The word literally means "chowder," but it's colloquially understood to mean "mixture of foods." You'll spend little time in preparation, and a lot of time enjoying.

2 ounces cellophane
  noodles
4 10¾-ounce cans
  chicken broth
1½ cans water
2 medium carrots, cut
  into ⅛-inch rounds
¾ pound medium
  shrimp, shelled and
  deveined
8 ounces fish fillets, cut
  into 1-inch pieces (best
  if haddock, cod, scrod,
  or orange roughy)
4 ounces snowpeas
1 tablespoon soy sauce
12 fresh mushrooms,
  thinly sliced
4 green onions, cut into
  1½-inch pieces
  (tops included)

1 Before starting to cook, cover the noodles with hot water in a small saucepan or bowl and let stand 8 to 10 minutes. Drain and cut into 2-inch lengths.

2 Place the chicken broth, water, and carrots in a Dutch oven or stockpot and heat to boiling, then reduce the heat and simmer uncovered for 5 minutes. Stir in the noodles and all remaining ingredients. Cover and heat to boiling, then reduce heat and simmer until the shrimp are coral pink and the fish flakes easily, 3 to 5 minutes.

Stock Some Stock

Keep a few cans of chicken and beef broth handy. Most commercial brands are excellent, and when time is of the essence, will adequately serve you. When you have a little extra time, make some of your own and freeze it.

Chicken Stew

A quick and hearty way to use up leftover chicken. A staple in the Bowersox household, though the recipe hails from my mother's side of the family, the Fredericks of West Virginia.

1 tablespoon vege-
  table oil
1 small onion, diced
⅛ teaspoon garlic
  powder
1 teaspoon dried beef
  bouillon
2½ pounds boneless
  chicken, skinned and
  cut into bite-size pieces
4 medium tomatoes,
  diced
1½ cups water
1 cup diced carrots
1 cup sliced fresh
  mushrooms
2 teaspoons chopped
  dried tarragon
Salt and pepper to taste
2 tablespoons flour

1 In a skillet or small stockpot over medium-high heat, combine the oil, onion, garlic powder, bouillon mix, and chicken. Cook, stirring occasionally, until the chicken is cooked through and beginning to brown, about 3 minutes.

2 Add the tomatoes, water, carrots, mushrooms, tarragon, and salt and pepper. Bring to a boil, then reduce the heat and simmer 5 minutes.

3 In a small bowl or mixing cup, combine 2 tablespoons of the broth from the stockpot and 2 tablespoons of flour, and stir until blended. Add to the stew and stir until stew begins to thicken. If you wish the stew to be even thicker, repeat this step.

4 Serve hot with garlic bread.

Use Cleanup for One Meal to Save Time on the Next

Whenever you have leftovers—chicken, turkey, beef, ham—consider how you'll use them before storing them in the refrigerator for tomorrow. With a few minutes of effort during cleanup, you can save yourself a great deal of time on the next day's menu. Pick the chicken or turkey carcass, tearing the meat into bite-size chunks for your soup or salad plans for the next day. Cut the beef or ham into the strips or chunks for tomorrow's stir-fry or stew recipe. You'll not only save yourself time but also storage space in the refrigerator.

Cuban Chicken Stew

This is one of those many gems that come my way thanks to viewer generosity. It arrived following an edition of *In the Kitchen with Bob* that featured chicken stews and soups. I had mentioned that there was probably a different recipe for chicken stew for every nationality on earth. The viewer thought I might like to add her family's Cuban version to my repertoire. Absolutely! It's wonderful.

2½ pounds chicken pieces, a mix of breasts, thighs, and legs
1 tablespoon olive oil
1 medium onion, thinly sliced
½ red bell pepper, seeded and finely chopped
½ green bell pepper, seeded and finely chopped
2 garlic cloves, minced
¾ teaspoon dried oregano
¾ teaspoon ground cumin
1 15-ounce can tomato sauce
1 cup dry white wine
4 small red-skinned potatoes, quartered
½ cup raisins
½ cup pitted black olives
Salt and pepper to taste
1 cup shelled peas

 1 Preheat the oven to 375 degrees. Skin the chicken pieces and trim as much fat as possible.

2 In a wide frying pan over medium heat, heat the oil and add the chicken, cooking until it is well browned on all sides, about 3 to 5 minutes. Remove the pieces and transfer to a deep casserole dish.

3 Add the onion and bell peppers to the drippings left in the pan; add a little more olive oil if there isn't at least 1 tablespoon of drippings left. Stir in the garlic, oregano, and cumin. Sauté briefly, then add the tomato sauce and the wine. Cook, stirring often, until the sauce comes to a boil. Reduce heat and simmer for about 5 minutes.

4 Add the potatoes to the chicken in the casserole, then sprinkle in the raisins and olives, then salt and pepper. Pour the sauce over the chicken. Your work is now finished.

5 Bake, covered, for 1½ to 2 hours. Remove from heat long enough to stir in the peas, then bake another 10 minutes. Serve hot.

Classic Irish Stew

Makes 8 to 10 servings

History tells us that the original Irish stew was made from baby goat instead of sheep, because the latter was too valuable for peasants to eat. These days good lamb is as plentiful and affordable as beef, so we can enjoy the hearty, basic stew that carried many an Irishman through his day. Though there are as many recipes as there are Irish families, this one is the classic.

8 large potatoes, peeled and sliced ½ inch thick
6 large onions, sliced ¼ inch thick
4 pounds lean, boneless lamb, cut into 1-inch cubes
4 teaspoons salt (or more, if desired)
4 teaspoons freshly ground black pepper
½ teaspoon dried thyme

1 In a Dutch oven or stew pot, make a solid layer on the bottom with half the potatoes. On top of those make a layer with half the onions. Then arrange all the lamb chunks in a layer over the onions, and sprinkle the salt, pepper, and thyme over the lamb. Cover with the remaining onions, and top with the remaining potatoes.

2 Pour in enough cold water to just cover and bring to a boil. Simmer over low heat for about 1½ hours or until the vegetables and lamb are tender. Check the pot frequently. If the liquid is simmering away, add more water—a little at a time—so that you don't pull down the temperature in the pot all at once.

3 Serve in heated bowls, ladling directly out of the Dutch oven, which should be carried directly to the table, as the Irish would.

Note: You can bake this stew in a 350 degree oven if you prefer. Once you have brought the stew to a boil on top of the stove, just pop it into the preheated oven and bake. Check frequently as well, to make sure you're not losing too much liquid. The stew *must* simmer, so it thickens and all the flavors mingle in the pot.

Steak Stew

Growing up in Colorado meant that I saw steak on the table in some form at least three or four times a week. Though my father liked his barbecued on an open grill, my mother would get more creative. Sometimes she made this stew with any leftover beef she had from a roast, but often she shot the rest of the week's food budget on a great piece of top round or London broil, and made this rich stew infused with the mouthwatering flavor of good beef. My mother often used a package of frozen mixed vegetables, but I prefer fresh.

1 pound boneless top
 round steak or London
 broil, cut into bite-size
 cubes
5 tablespoons butter or
 margarine
⅓ cup flour
5 cups beef stock
½ cup diced celery
½ cup diced carrots
1 cup chopped onion
1 ½ cups cubed tomatoes
1 ½ teaspoons freshly
 ground black pepper
12 to 16 ounces mixed
 vegetables (broccoli or
 cauliflower flowerettes,
 corn kernels, cubed
 large potato, ½
 chopped green bell
 pepper and ½
 chopped red bell
 pepper, baby lima
 beans)
Salt and pepper to taste

1 In a 5-quart stockpot, Dutch oven, or stew pot, sauté the beef cubes in 2 tablespoons of the butter or margarine over medium-high heat until just browned on the outside and still rare to medium-rare on the inside. (If you like your beef more well done, sauté a minute or two longer.) Remove the beef and reserve, and drain any drippings, but leave in the browned bits.

2 Place the remaining 3 tablespoons of butter or margarine in the pot and melt without browning. Add the flour and stir constantly until you have a smooth paste. Slowly pour in the beef stock, stirring so the mixture remains smooth. It should thicken slightly.

3 Add the vegetables and bring the pot to a boil. Reduce heat, cover, and simmer for about 30 minutes. Add the beef cubes again, and simmer for another 15 minutes. Serve in a heated bowl with garlic bread on the side.

Vatapa
Brazilian Seafood Stew

Being a fan of many cuisines, one of my favorite cookbooks has been *Betty Crocker's New International Cookbook.* It truly covers the world and has been immensely helpful in putting together a number of *In the Kitchen with Bob* segments. This recipe caught my eye immediately. It combines the spiciness of Brazilian cooking with my great love, seafood. And it's creative use of things like coconut milk and peanut butter are intriguing. It's a snap to make as well!

1 large onion, thinly sliced

3 to 5 fresh green chilies, seeded and finely chopped

2 garlic cloves, chopped

½ teaspoon paprika

½ teaspoon hot red pepper flakes

5 or 6 tablespoons olive oil

3 cups coconut milk

1 16-ounce can whole tomatoes, drained and chopped

1½ teaspoons salt

5 ounces small shrimp, peeled, deveined, and minced

1 cup soft bread crumbs

1 cup smooth peanut butter

1 pound medium to large shrimp, peeled and deveined

1 pound cod fillets, cut into 1½-inch pieces

¼ cup fresh cilantro, snipped

1 16-ounce jar medium to hot salsa

1 In a large stockpot over medium heat, cook the onion, chilies, garlic, paprika, and red pepper flakes in 2 tablespoons of the olive oil. Cook, stirring, until the onion is tender and translucent, about 3 minutes. Stir in the coconut milk, tomatoes, salt, and small shrimp. Heat to boiling, then reduce the heat and simmer uncovered for 15 minutes.

2 Stir in the bread crumbs and peanut butter until well blended and the mixture is thickened. Keep this mixture warm.

3 In a 10-inch skillet, heat 3 remaining tablespoons of olive oil over medium heat. Cook the shrimp until coral pink, about 2 minutes, stirring. Remove the shrimp with a slotted spoon and add to the sauce in the stockpot.

4 Add a little more oil to the skillet if necessary, and add the fish until it flakes easily when touched with a fork, about 2 minutes. Gently stir the fish into the stew mixture and cook another 1 to 2 minutes.

5 Serve stew hot in heated bowls, sprinkled with cilantro. Serve hot salsa on the side for diners to add to stew as they wish.

Crabmeat Stew

Makes 6 servings

1 pound crabmeat,
  cleaned
½ cup dry sherry
2 tablespoons butter or
  margarine
¼ cup chopped green
  onion (including tops)
3 tablespoons chopped
  green bell pepper
2 garlic cloves, minced
1 ½ tablespoons flour
½ teaspoon dried
  rosemary
¾ cup peeled and
  chopped tomatoes
1 teaspoon salt
¼ teaspoon freshly
  ground black pepper
1 cup heavy cream
French bread, cut into
  1- or 2-inch rounds,
  toasted

I inherited this twist on a chowder with my father's treasure trove of recipes. Heartier than a soup or a bisque, it will delight any crab lover.

1 Before cooking, combine the crabmeat and sherry in a bowl and refrigerate for about 1 hour.

2 Melt the butter or margarine in a skillet over medium heat. Sauté the green onion, green pepper, and garlic until crisp-tender, about 1 to 2 minutes. Blend in the flour and rosemary, then add the tomatoes, salt, and pepper. Reduce heat to low, and cook for 5 minutes.

3 Stir in the cream and the crabmeat, including the sherry. Cook another 5 minutes. Serve in heated bowls with toasted French bread rounds.

An Easy Way to Thinly Slice an Onion Safely

When asked to thinly slice an onion, most of us peel it and try to hold it steady while using our chef's blade to slice it. The problem is, an onion is round and it tends to want to roll, making it a bit more difficult and dangerous than it has to be. Simply cut off a 1-inch slice from one end of the onion. Stand the onion on that now-flat surface, and cut down through the onion in thin slices. Though your slices won't necessarily be complete rings, most recipes don't require that, and you'll be eliminating the potential for problems.

Bouillabaisse

Bouillabaisse is one of the many gifts the Marseilles area of France has given the world. This version of the classic fish stew was made every Christmas Eve by a novelist friend of mine who would invite a close-knit group of friends to enjoy a warm fire, lively conversation, a good wine or two, and her superb Bouillabaisse. Because of the fond memories of those evenings, Bouillabaisse is one thing I always consider for informal gatherings of friends.

3 tablespoons olive oil
1 medium onion, chopped
3 medium tomatoes, peeled, seeded, and chopped
2 garlic cloves, minced
Bouquet garni of 1 bay leaf and ⅛ teaspoon each of dried thyme, dried basil, dried tarragon, chives, chopped parsley
Salt and pepper to taste
Pinch of saffron
3½ cups boiling water
1½ cups boiling clam juice
2 to 3 pounds mixed fish fillets and shellfish (½ pound halibut, ½ pound cod, ½ pound red snapper, ½ pound lobster, ½ pound medium shrimp, 1 dozen mussels)
½ cup dry white wine
8 slices French bread
2 tablespoons finely chopped fresh parsley

1 Heat the olive oil in a stockpot over medium-high heat. Add the onion and cook until softened, stirring occasionally, about 1 to 2 minutes. Add the tomatoes, garlic, and bouquet garni. Season with the salt and pepper and the saffron and blend well.

2 Add the boiling water and clam juice, then immediately add firm-fleshed fish. Bring to a boil, then add the shrimp and lobster, soft-fleshed fish, and the wine. Continue cooking and stir occasionally to keep fish from sinking to the bottom and sticking until fish begins to break apart. Remove bouquet garni.

3 Place a piece of bread in each serving bowl, and surround it with a variety of the fish and shellfish. Then ladle the broth over all. Sprinkle parsley over the top. Serve hot with extra French bread.

Oyster Stew

Makes 4 to 6 servings

2 pints shucked oysters, with liquid
6 cups light cream
2 cups milk, scalded
¼ teaspoon cayenne pepper
1 teaspoon salt
2 tablespoons butter or margarine
Paprika

This is as simple as it gets, and is truly for the oyster lover—there are no other flavors intruding.

1 Pour off the liquid from the oysters and reserve.

2 In a bowl, blend the cream, milk, cayenne pepper, and salt. Set aside.

3 In a medium stockpot or Dutch oven, melt the butter or margarine over medium heat and add the oysters. Cook gently, stirring once or twice, until the oysters plump. Pour in the reserved oyster liquid and the cream mixture. Heat until the oysters are cooked through, but not overcooked, about 10 minutes. (They'll become tough if you overcook them.)

4 Serve in heated bowls, sprinkled lightly with paprika.

Philippine Stew

What I like about this stew is the distinctly oriental flavor it has, and the interesting mix of chicken and sausage. I'm also very partial to tarragon. Though I can't trace how this recipe came to me, I like making this stew because it doesn't require a large number of steps spread over a longer period of time. It's quick, but complex enough not to taste like it.

10 ounces mildly hot sausage, without casings, crumbled
1 medium onion, chopped
5 garlic cloves, minced
1 14-ounce can chicken broth
1 14-ounce can chopped peeled tomatoes, drained
3 cups water
1 bay leaf
½ teaspoon ground ginger
¾ teaspoon chopped dried tarragon
1 ½ pounds boneless, skinless chicken breasts, cut into 1 ½-inch chunks
1 8-ounce can garbanzo beans, drained
2 sweet potatoes, peeled and sliced ½ inch thick
1 cup white rice
½ pound bok choy, washed and shredded (both tops and stalks)
2 firm bananas, sliced
3 green onions, sliced (including tops)

1 In a Dutch oven or small stockpot, break up the sausage with a spoon and cook over medium heat. When browned, add the onion and cook, stirring, until the onion is softened, about 1 to 2 minutes.

2 Add the garlic, chicken broth, tomatoes, water, bay leaf, ginger, tarragon, chicken, garbanzo beans, sweet potatoes, and rice. Heat to boiling, then reduce to a comfortable simmer over medium-low heat. Simmer for 30 to 40 minutes.

3 Stir in the bok choy and bananas. Cover and cook for another 10 minutes. Remove bay leaf. Serve in heated bowls, with a sprinkling of green onion on top.

Crepe Chalet Jambalaya

Makes 6 to 8 servings

2 cups finely chopped
  onions
2 tablespoons olive oil
1½ cups finely chopped
  celery
4 cloves garlic, minced
2 cups chopped green
  bell pepper
½ cup chopped red bell
  pepper
1½ pounds cooked ham,
  sliced ½ inch thick
2 bay leaves
½ teaspoon chopped
  fresh thyme (3 sprigs)
1 16-ounce can Italian
  plum tomatoes
½ cup finely chopped
  fresh parsley
Salt and freshly ground
  black pepper to taste
Tabasco sauce to taste
2 cups clam juice
2 cups water
1½ cups quick-cooking
  whole-grain rice
  (like Uncle Ben's)
2½ pounds medium
  shrimp, peeled and
  deveined
¾ pound bay scallops
½ quart shucked
  oysters, with liquid
  (optional)

Jambalaya was one of the most popular items on the menu at my restaurant, The Crepe Chalet. This version of the Cajun favorite was created by Xavier Teixido, one of the chefs at the Chalet. He had studied and worked under several of New Orleans's best, and this recipe is one of the many standouts he brought with him.

1 In a Dutch oven or large stockpot, cook the onions in the olive oil over medium-high heat until translucent, about 1 to 2 minutes. Add the celery, garlic, and bell peppers, and cook another 3 minutes or so.

2 Cut the ham into ½-inch cubes and add it to the pot; add the bay leaves, thyme, tomatoes, parsley, salt and pepper, and Tabasco. The more Tabasco, the spicier your Jambalaya—use your own judgment. Stir frequently and cook for 2 minutes.

3 Add half the clam juice and half the water. Simmer for 10 minutes. Stir frequently to pull up ingredients from the bottom of the pot, so nothing burns. Add the rice, then cover and cook for another 10 minutes.

4 Add the rest of the clam juice and water, the shrimp, and the scallops (and oysters, if you include them). Cook for another 10 to 15 minutes, stirring. Make sure you stir frequently, pulling all ingredients up from the bottom. Add more liquid (a mixture of broth and water) to keep stew from drying out too much or burning. Remove bay leaves. Serve in heated bowls with Tabasco on the side.

Jambalaya Louis Armstrong

Makes about 8 servings

2 tablespoons butter or margarine
2 cups chopped onions
⅓ cup sliced green onions
⅔ cup chopped green bell pepper
1 tablespoon minced garlic
2 tablespoons minced fresh parsley
½ pound lean boneless pork, cut into ½-inch cubes
1 cup cubed chicken breast, in ½-inch pieces
1 cup cubed baked ham, in ½-inch pieces
Cayenne pepper to taste (the more you add, the spicier it gets)
½ teaspoon chili powder
2 bay leaves, crushed
¼ teaspoon dried thyme
⅛ teaspoon ground cloves
⅛ teaspoon ground cumin
⅛ teaspoon ground allspice
Salt and pepper to taste
6 smoked garlic sausages, cut into ½-inch slices
3 cups beef stock
1½ cups quick-cooking whole-grain rice (like Uncle Ben's)
1½ pounds medium shrimp, peeled and deveined

Thanks to viewer Kate Linde for sending this recipe to me. She is a great jazz lover as well as a QVC regular, and when jazz great Louis Armstrong visited her town years ago, she invited him for dinner. He accepted, but with the stipulation that he do the cooking himself. This is the recipe for Jambalaya that he prepared that evening for Kate and her family. Mr. Armstrong said that his family's version of this Cajun delight came from Gonzales, Louisiana, near New Orleans.

1 In an 8- or 12-quart stockpot over medium heat, combine the butter, onions, green onions, green pepper, garlic, parsley, pork, chicken, and ham. Cook, stirring, until meat and vegetables are lightly browned, about 5 minutes.

2 Add the cayenne, chili powder, bay leaves, thyme, cloves, cumin, allspice, salt, and pepper. Cook another 5 minutes, stirring frequently. Add the sausage and cook for 5 to 10 minutes more.

3 Add the stock and rice, bring to a boil, then turn heat down and cook for 40 minutes, uncovered. Add the shrimp during the last 10 minutes. Continue to stir frequently, pulling the ingredients up from the bottom of the stockpot. When the shrimp are coral color, the Jambalaya is ready to serve. Serve in heated bowls, with cayenne pepper and Tabasco on the table to "hot it up," as Louis said.

Bayou Gumbo

Makes 10 to 12 servings

ROUX
1 ½ cups vegetable oil
2 cups all-purpose flour

GUMBO
2 green bell peppers,
  seeded and chopped
2 large, spicy onions,
  chopped
1 medium chicken, cut
  into pieces and
  deboned
1 pound smoked
  sausage, cut into
  ½-inch pieces
2 medium zucchini, cut
  into ⅛-inch slices
½ pound okra, sliced
4 quarts water
2 cups chicken stock
¼ cup hot sauce
  ("summer" sauce,
  Jamaican Hot Sauce,
  Tabasco, any
  commercial gumbo
  sauce)
3 tablespoons Cajun
  seasoning
Salt and pepper to taste
1 pound shrimp, peeled
  and deveined
1 pint shucked oysters
  (optional)
Cooked rice

Gumbo gets its name from the African word for okra, *quingumbo.* Its seeds were brought to America with the slave trade. Okra is a green vegetable that has thickening capabilities, and is therefore an essential part of any gumbo. The other essential is a *roux,* a mix of oil and flour that is cooked until richly browned. It not only thickens the stew, as the okra does, but also adds most of the familiar flavor, whether the gumbo is based on fish or fowl. The longer the roux is browned, the richer and more flavorful the gumbo becomes. These are delicious, hearty stews, and this version is one of the most requested recipes I've prepared on *In the Kitchen with Bob.*

1 In a large stockpot, prepare the roux. Heat the oil over medium-high heat and sprinkle in the flour a little at a time, stirring constantly to ensure smoothness. Reduce the heat to medium-low and cook, stirring often, until roux has become a rich, nutty brown, about 5 minutes. Constantly scrape the bottom of the pan to pull up all the bits.

2 Add the green peppers and onions, and cook until they are soft, about 2 to 3 minutes. Then add the chicken, sausage, zucchini, okra, water, stock, hot sauce, Cajun seasoning, and salt and pepper. Bring to a boil, stirring well, so that nothing sits on the bottom of the pan for too long. Reduce the heat and simmer for about 1 hour.

3 Add the shrimp (and oysters, if desired). Return the gumbo to a boil, and cook for about 5 minutes or until shrimp are coral. Serve over rice, with a bottle of hot sauce on the table.

Turkey Chili

Makes 3 to 4 servings

This is a great way for chili lovers to dig into a bowl of their favorite concoction without all the fat and cholesterol. It's every bit as robust as a beef chili, and like a beef chili, gets better as the leftovers are heated and reheated.

1 tablespoon oil

⅔ cup chopped green
bell pepper

3 to 4 garlic cloves,
minced

1 medium to large onion,
finely chopped

1 pound ground turkey

2 medium to large
tomatoes, chopped

1 10¾-ounce can kidney
beans, drained

1 16-ounce can tomato
sauce

2 tablespoons soy sauce

2 tablespoons chili
powder (this amount
will make it
medium-hot)

½ teaspoon ground
cumin

½ teaspoon dried sage

½ teaspoon dried thyme

¼ cup chopped onion
(as garnish)

1 lime, cut into wedges
(as garnish)

1 In a 3-quart saucepan, heat the oil over medium-high heat. Add the green pepper, garlic, and onion. Stir and cook until the onion is wilted, about 1 to 2 minutes.

2 Increase heat to high. Add the turkey to the pan, break it up with a spoon, and cook, stirring gently, until it begins to brown. Add the remaining ingredients. Stir well, making sure you scrape up any browned bits on the bottom of the pot. Reduce the heat, cover, and simmer for 30 minutes.

3 Serve in heated bowls, with chopped onions sprinkled on top. Offer the lime wedges to squeeze over the chili as desired.

Keep 'em Handy

Always keep your seasonings, herbs, and spices within easy reach of where you're working. If you have the time before cooking, measure them out for your recipe. You'll save a lot of time in searching and movement about the kitchen.

Pedernales River Chili
(LBJ Chili)

Makes 10 to 12 servings

This is an original chili created by former President Lyndon Baines Johnson. He named it after his ranch, which stretched along the Pedernales River in Texas. It was served on many a night while Johnson occupied the White House. I was sent the recipe by a viewer, and recently have found it in Bernard Clayton, Jr.'s wonderful book of soups and stews as well. The masa harina—the Mexican cornmeal used to make tortillas—is Bernard's addition to the original LBJ recipe. It acts as a thickener in a stew, and is a good addition, as President Johnson, unlike most chili lovers, preferred his chili thin.

1 ½ cups chopped onions
1 to 2 garlic cloves, minced
1 tablespoon oil (LBJ preferred bacon drippings)
2 pounds coarsely ground beef
½ teaspoon dried oregano
1 teaspoon finely ground cumin seeds
2 to 3 tablespoons chili powder ("depends on your tolerance for heat," according to LBJ)
2 cups crushed tomatoes
Salt to taste
1 cup beef stock, warmed
⅓ cup masa harina (or cornmeal)

1 In a large skillet or small stockpot, sauté the onions and garlic in the oil over high heat until tender and translucent, about 1 to 2 minutes. Add the beef, breaking up any large chunks. Stir it frequently, so it browns thoroughly.

2 Reduce the heat, and sprinkle in the oregano, cumin, and chili powder. Stir again and continue cooking for 3 to 5 minutes. Add the tomatoes and the salt.

3 Place the heated beef stock in a small mixing bowl, and slowly add the masa harina. Stir until blended, then add to the chili. Bring to a boil, then reduce heat and simmer for about 1 hour. Stir the chili frequently to ensure that flavors mingle.

4 Serve in bowls with a thick-crusted Italian-style bread.

Vegetarian Chili

Makes 6 servings

This is another of the most requested recipes I've prepared on *In the Kitchen with Bob*. I found the original in Sunset's *Vegetarian Cooking*, but have arrived at this version through a couple years of experimentation. I've had a number of viewers write me as to how well it's been received by the chili lovers in their families. For as robust a flavor as it has, it's remarkable that it has almost no fat.

4 large onions, chopped
1 large green bell
   pepper, seeded and
   chopped
3 tablespoons oil
1 tablespoon mustard
   seeds
2 to 3 tablespoons chili
   powder (according to
   your taste for a spicy
   chili)
1 teaspoon cumin seeds
1 ½ teaspoons
   unsweetened cocoa
¼ teaspoon ground
   cinnamon
1 pound canned
   tomatoes, crushed
1 6-ounce can tomato
   paste
2 16-ounce cans kidney
   beans, undrained
½ cup water
Salt to taste
4 to 6 dashes Tabasco
   sauce (again, according
   to your taste for spicy)
Limes, cut into wedges
   (as garnish)

1 In a Dutch oven or larger stockpot, sauté the onions and green pepper in the oil over medium-high heat until onions are browned, about 2 to 3 minutes. Add the mustard seeds and cook for 1 minute, stirring constantly.

2 Add the chili powder, cumin seeds, cocoa, cinnamon, tomatoes, and tomato paste. Cook for 1 to 2 minutes. Add the kidney beans, water, salt, and Tabasco. Your work is now finished. Reduce heat and simmer vigorously, uncovered, for about 40 minutes, or until the chili has thickened. Stir frequently to prevent scorching.

3 Serve in heated bowls. Squeeze the juice of 1 or 2 lime wedges into the chili just before eating.

Maintain a Well-Stocked Spice Cabinet

Always try to keep your spice cabinet stocked and fresh. Nothing will slow you down more than having to run to the market for a spice you thought you had.

Salads, Appetizers, and Hors d'Oeuvres

S alads are our direct connection to the earth. We seldom adulterate the bounty of fruits and vegetables we use to make our salads, and they are therefore a marvelous natural blend of fresh flavors and nutrients. They allow for such a wide range of creativity; no matter what you try, there's really no wrong mix or styling. I find them great fun.

I've always viewed salads—and most appetizers—as a bridge from soup to entree: a light, refreshing passage that complements each. But I also like salads to have the ability to stand alone, if need be, such as the spinach-rich Korean Salad, Chopped Antipasto, or Toni's Broccoli Salad included here. Unusual combinations, such as the Cashew, Shrimp, and Pea Salad or Hot Shrimp Salad, make a terrific light lunch, and the brightness of the Mandarin Orange Salad is perfect anytime, anywhere.

Appetizers should be able to stand alone as

well. Many's the time I've enjoyed just a soup and appetizer for dinner, and most of those included here would serve well. For the seafood lovers, I recommend the Scallops in White Wine or Sherried Clams, and for those with a penchant for the hot and spicy, the Shrimp Cocktail with Ata Sauce will offer the heat you're looking for.

I've found the appetizers I've included can also be great hors d'oeuvres as well, especially the Beef Chaing Mai, my father's Authentic Quiche Lorraine, and the One-Dish Crab Dip. And I guarantee you've never had any finger food quite as addicting as the Oysterette Munchies.

Cashew, Shrimp, and Pea Salad

Makes 4 servings

My first experience with this refreshing salad recipe came as a result of my wife, Toni's love of cashews. I wanted something light and quick for a summer lunch, and I found it in Sunset's *Quick & Easy Cook Book.* It was such a hit with her that I tried it on *In the Kitchen with Bob,* and was inundated with requests for the recipe. It's a meal in itself, but I also think it can be a wonderful buffet dish in larger quantities.

DILL DRESSING
¼ cup mayonnaise
¼ cup sour cream
1 tablespoon lemon juice
1 tablespoon minced fresh dill or 1 teaspoon dried dill

1 ½ cups roasted cashews (salted or unsalted)
1 16-ounce package fresh or frozen baby peas, defrosted and drained
1 cup thinly sliced green onions (including tops)
2 large celery stalks, cut diagonally into thin slices
¾ pound small shrimp, peeled, deveined, and cooked
Salt and pepper to taste
6 to 8 large butter lettuce leaves, rinsed and chilled
Dill sprigs (as garnish)

1 Prepare the dressing by mixing all ingredients in a medium bowl. Set aside in the refrigerator.

2 In a large bowl, combine the cashews, peas, green onions, celery, and shrimp. Toss to mix.

3 Add the dressing and mix thoroughly. Season with salt and pepper and toss gently again.

4 Line a plate or shallow soup bowl with the lettuce leaves so they form a kind of pocket or bowl. Spoon the salad into the center of the leaves. Toss a few more cashews on top, and add a couple of dill sprigs as garnish. Refrigerate until ready to serve.

Mandarin Orange Salad

Makes 6 to 8 servings

The Bowersox kids grew up with this salad always on the second shelf of the refrigerator. It was my mother's creation as far as I know, and she was never without some ready. It's a particularly refreshing salad, and a perfect touch for a light dinner party. You're going to get dozens of requests for this one.

1 8-ounce container Cool Whip

1 17-ounce can pineapple chunks, drained

1 17-ounce can mandarin orange slices, drained

1 24-ounce container cottage cheese

1 6-ounce package orange-flavored Jell-O

1 Combine all ingredients in a large mixing bowl and stir together thoroughly. Do this gently, so as not to break up the fruit.

2 Place in a mold of your choice and let set in the refrigerator for several hours before serving.

Bowls

Invest in two sets of bowls. The first should be a nested series of 3 to 5 stainless-steel bowls. They are virtually indestructible, and may just be one of the most useful tools in the kitchen. The second should be a 3- to 5-bowl series of tempered glass, either clear or patterned. They are perfect for so many things, including serving most salads.

Korean Salad

This has been a summer staple in my home for nearly twenty years. The recipe came to me by way of my brother-in-law, Ken Morris, a hardy Coloradan who enjoys the health and energy good salads impart. Personally, I think it's the dressing that makes the salad—I've often thought of bottling it myself. It's marvelous.

1 10-ounce bag spinach, washed and torn
¼ pound bacon, browned and crumbled
1 6- to 8-ounce bag fresh bean sprouts
1 6-ounce can water chestnuts, sliced
4 or 5 hard-boiled eggs, sliced, yolks discarded

DRESSING
⅓ cup sugar or honey
⅓ cup catsup
1 tablespoon Worcestershire sauce
2 teaspoons salt
1 cup vegetable oil
¼ cup cider vinegar
¾ medium onion, chopped

1 In a large bowl, mix all the ingredients for the salad.

2 For the dressing, put all the ingredients in a blender and blend until very smooth. We like to place the dressing in the freezer for 5 to 10 minutes before serving, but you can use it immediately. The dressing will keep in the refrigerator for up to a week.

3 Place the salad mix on individual plates, and spoon personal amounts of dressing over each.

Chopped Antipasto

The chopped antipasto is great as a single course or as a complete meal. Here's a version I've been working on for over ten years. It changes a little every time I make it. I started out trying to match an outstanding offering served by a small family-run Italian restaurant near my home, but now the recipe has become an ever-changing palette for experimentation—change a little of this, change a little of that, see what happens. I'll give you my starting point. See where *you* can take it.

1 average head iceberg lettuce
1 small head romaine lettuce
2 medium tomatoes
½ 6- to 8-ounce jar green olives
½ 10-ounce can ripe (black) olives
½ 6- to 8-ounce jar sweet peppers
½ red bell pepper
½ green bell pepper
½ yellow bell pepper
4 celery stalks
1 large onion
¼ pound salami, thinly sliced
¼ pound boiled ham, thinly sliced
¼ pound prosciutto, thinly sliced
¼ pound provolone cheese, thinly sliced
¼ cup olive oil
¼ cup red wine vinegar
Grated Parmesan cheese

1 Chop each salad ingredient finely and add to a large bowl. Mix well.

2 Pour the olive oil and vinegar over the salad and toss well. Serve with sliced Italian bread and grated Parmesan.

Keep a Sharp Edge

Keep your cutlery as sharp as possible. It makes for faster and safer work. It might pay to invest in a high-quality sharpener, so that you can put a professional edge on any knife in seconds simply by drawing the blade through the machine.

Toni's Broccoli Salad

Makes 6 to 8 servings

I call this the "cousin salad." My wife, Toni, was given the recipe by one of her cousins, who received it from *her* cousin, who received it from . . . you get the idea. It's always been given rave reviews by anyone who's tried it, and we never go to picnics or family reunions without it. Another great side dish or full meal salad.

DRESSING

2 cups mayonnaise
½ cup sugar
**6 tablespoons apple
 cider vinegar**

**16 slices cooked bacon
 (roughly 1 pound),
 drained**
**8 cups broccoli
 flowerettes, washed
 and drained**
**1 large Bermuda onion,
 chopped**
½ cup raisins

1 In a bowl, mix the dressing ingredients thoroughly and set aside.

2 In a large skillet, cook the bacon until crisp. Drain bacon between sheets of absorbent paper towels, so as to pull as much grease from the bacon as possible.

3 In a large bowl, combine the remaining salad ingredients. Add the bacon and dressing, and toss thoroughly.

Western Sauerkraut Salad

This is an old family favorite. If you love sauerkraut, you'll find it mouthwatering. I once tried to make the sauerkraut from scratch, but I don't recommend it. There are plenty of good brands in the market.

1 20-ounce bag sauerkraut
1 ½ cups chopped pimientos
1 medium onion, finely chopped
1 medium carrot, shredded
¼ cup vegetable oil
1 cup sugar
½ cup cider vinegar
Salt to taste

1 Rinse the brine from the sauerkraut with cold water, drain in a colander, then place in a large salad bowl. Add the rest of the vegetables and mix.

2 In a small bowl, combine the oil, sugar, vinegar, and salt. Mix well, then add to the sauerkraut and vegetables.

3 Toss well, then let the salad stand in the refrigerator for about 1 hour before serving.

Mushroom Salad

Mushrooms always seem to be part of the chorus line, never the star, which to me has been a matter of role and costuming rather than talent. I love mushrooms, and this recipe brings the mushroom center stage. It's been in the family files for decades, but we saw it only on those occasions that called for buffet-style offerings. I think it deserves more exposure. It has a gourmet look and taste, and can add a welcome difference to a dinner party.

1 ½ pounds fresh button mushrooms
1 teaspoon lemon juice
⅓ cup vegetable oil (with a touch of olive oil added)
½ cup red wine vinegar
2 garlic cloves, crushed
3 teaspoons sugar
1 ½ teaspoons salt
⅛ teaspoon freshly ground black pepper
⅛ teaspoon dried oregano
Dash of Tabasco sauce (optional)
Butter lettuce leaves, washed, drained, and crisped

1 Wash the mushrooms well. Put into boiling water with the lemon juice for 2 to 3 minutes. Drain immediately. (The lemon juice helps keep the mushrooms white.)

2 In a large bowl, combine the mushrooms with all the other ingredients (including the Tabasco, if desired). Mix well.

3 Cover and refrigerate overnight. Stir several times when you can, especially just before serving. Serve on 1 or 2 butter lettuce leaves arranged as a kind of bowl on a salad plate.

Marinated Vegetable Salad

A colorful and tangy salad that can also serve as a relish, this is a great recipe to have around for those last-minute entertaining situations.

1 17-ounce can white shoe-peg corn, or use frozen
1 17-ounce can green beans, drained and chopped, or use frozen
1 17-ounce can baby peas, drained, or use frozen
1 small green bell pepper, chopped
1 small onion, finely chopped
1 cup finely chopped celery
½ cup oil
¾ cup red wine vinegar
¾ cup sugar
1 teaspoon salt
1 teaspoon pepper
1 tablespoon water

1 In a large bowl, combine the corn, green beans, baby peas, green pepper, onion, and celery.

2 In another bowl, combine the oil, vinegar, sugar, salt, pepper, and water. Stir until the sugar has dissolved. Pour over the vegetables and toss.

3 Marinate the salad in the refrigerator for several hours before serving.

Hot Shrimp Salad

Makes 4 to 6 servings

2 tablespoons vege-
   table oil
1 pound medium shrimp,
   peeled and deveined
2 tablespoons roughly
   chopped fresh parsley
4 green onions (with
   tops), thinly sliced
2 medium tomatoes,
   seeded and chopped
½ teaspoon salt
2 garlic cloves, finely
   chopped
8 drops aromatic bitters
⅓ cup lime juice
⅛ teaspoon hot red
   pepper flakes
1 avocado, peeled and
   chopped
Butter lettuce leaves
Lime wedges (as garnish)

This is a versatile salad that can be served hot right after preparation, or refrigerated and served cold at a later time. Either way, it makes a great single meal.

1 In a large skillet, heat the oil and add the shrimp. As soon as the shrimp begin to turn coral, add the green onions, tomatoes, parsley, salt, and garlic. Stir briefly and cook for 1 minute.

2 Add the bitters, lime juice, and red pepper flakes. Stir. Gently add the avocado. Cover and remove from heat.

3 Cover the center of the serving plates with lettuce leaves. Spoon the shrimp mixture onto the lettuce and garnish with lime wedges. Serve warm immediately or refrigerate for serving later.

A Quick Peel

Here's a quick and easy way to peel a clove of garlic: Place the clove on a flat surface or cutting board. Gently place the flat side of a large kitchen knife, such as a chef's knife or oriental cleaver, on the clove and firmly smack the blade with the heel of your hand. The garlic peel will split and the clove will slide out easily.

Sherried Clams

Makes 3 to 4 servings

This is a wonderfully easy appetizer to make, and for the clam lover, an ambrosia of a recipe. I've adapted it from a recipe served in a local *tapas* bar, but its origins are in Spain, where some of the finest sherries are made. Though it takes little time to prepare, it has a rich and complex flavor, owing to the sherry.

2 tablespoons olive oil
1 small Spanish onion,
  finely chopped
½ cup cubed sugar-cured
  ham (⅛-inch pieces)
3 tablespoons semisweet
  sherry
1 10-ounce can littleneck
  clams, drained

1 In a large skillet, heat the oil over medium-high heat. Add the onion and sauté slowly, until the onion is wilted, about 1 to 2 minutes.

2 Add the ham, cooking for about 2 minutes, then the sherry and the clams. Cook the mixture for another 5 minutes, stirring the clams frequently to cover them with sauce. Serve on a bed of lettuce on an appetizer plate.

Scallops in White Wine

Makes 6 servings

Scallops are one of my favorite seafoods. I think their texture is unique in the world of foods, and I find them extremely versatile. They are also quick-cooking, and easily lend themselves to elegance in taste and presentation without forcing you into hours of meticulous preparation. This is a fine appetizer for a seafood or beef dinner, but in larger portions can very nicely stand by itself as an entree.

½ cup dry white wine
1 teaspoon white wine vinegar
1 medium carrot, julienned
4 thin onion slices, cut in half
1 celery stalk, julienned
2 bay leaves
½ teaspoon dried thyme
2 whole cloves
Salt and freshly ground pepper to taste
1 pound bay scallops, or sea scallops cut in half
4 teaspoons butter or margarine
4 teaspoons minced fresh parsley

1 In a small saucepan, combine the wine, vinegar, carrot, onion, celery, bay leaves, thyme, cloves, salt, and pepper. Bring to a boil, then reduce heat and simmer until sauce is reduced by about 10 percent (no more than 5 to 8 minutes).

2 Add the scallops and simmer for another 5 minutes. Remove the scallops when their flesh is white and firm. Keep them warm. Remove bay leaves from pan.

3 Combine the remaining sauce with the margarine and parsley, and blend thoroughly. Return the scallops to the sauce and stir well until hot again. Place the scallops in scallop shells and serve.

Mushrooms in Garlic Sauce

This is a classic, in both taste and ease of preparation. There are many recipes for mushrooms and garlic, but this is special. I found it in the marvelous book *Tapas* by Penelope Casas and altered it slightly to accommodate my zealous love of garlic and my presentation sensibilities. It's a breeze to make and serves well as an appetizer or hors d'oeuvre.

3 tablespoons olive oil
½ pound fresh
  mushrooms (button or
  larger), stems trimmed
  (quarter the
  mushrooms, if larger)
5 garlic cloves, thinly
  sliced
2 teaspoons lemon juice
3 tablespoons dry sherry
2 tablespoons chicken
  broth
2 tablespoons beef broth
½ teaspoon paprika
¼ teaspoon hot red
  pepper flakes
Salt and freshly ground
  pepper to taste
1 tablespoon minced
  fresh parsley
Butter lettuce leaves
Lemon wedges
  (as garnish)

1 Over high heat, heat the oil in a skillet until very hot. Add the mushrooms and garlic and sauté for 2 minutes.

2 Lower the heat and stir in the lemon juice, sherry, broths, paprika, red pepper flakes, salt, and pepper. Simmer another 1 to 3 minutes. Sprinkle with parsley and serve on butter lettuce leaves with a wedge of lemon.

Beef Chaing Mai

Makes 24 to 30 appetizers or hors d'oeuvres

One of the quickest ways to get something to your guests is to have them do most of the work. Beef Chaing Mai is a great participatory appetizer or hors d'oeuvre that lets your guests create their own mouthwatering little meat bundles. It's perfect for today's "everybody in the act" dinner parties, and very little time is needed to get it ready. The original recipe is Thai; this version is a mix of one found in the Sunset line of cookbooks and some fine-tuning of my own.

1 pound lean ground beef

¼ cup wild rice, finely ground in a chopper-grinder or blender

2 teaspoons sugar

1 teaspoon hot red pepper flakes

½ cup sliced green onions, including tops

½ cup chopped fresh mint leaves

2 tablespoons chopped fresh cilantro

¼ cup lemon juice

2 tablespoons soy sauce

1 teaspoon hot oriental sesame oil

Salt and pepper to taste

2 large heads butter lettuce, outer leaves discarded

Fresh mint sprigs

1 In a skillet, cook the ground beef until crumbled and no longer pink, about 5 minutes.

2 Stir in the rice, sugar, red pepper flakes, onions, green mint, cilantro, lemon juice, soy sauce, sesame oil, and salt and pepper. Heat through, stirring frequently to blend flavors.

3 Pour the beef mixture into a serving dish (or heated chafing dish) set in the center of a large round or oval platter. Surround the serving dish with the lettuce leaves and mint sprigs.

4 Guests spoon a small amount of the beef mixture onto the lettuce leaves, top it with a spring of mint, and roll it up to eat.

Authentic Quiche Lorraine

Makes 4 to 6 large servings, up to 10 hors d'oeuvres

1 Pillsbury Ready-Made Pie Crust (found in the dairy section)
6 strips bacon, cooked and cut into ½-inch squares
1 teaspoon butter or margarine
2 large shallots, finely chopped
2 eggs, plus 2 egg yolks
1 cup heavy cream
Salt and pepper to taste
Grated nutmeg

Quiche is actually a form of sixteenth-century flan, originating in the Lorraine region of France. While most of us think of quiche as including cheese, a traditional Quiche Lorraine does not use it. This version takes very little time to prepare because it uses a Pillsbury Ready-Made Pie Crust, which is very good and saves all the time of making a crust from scratch.

1 Preheat the oven to 375 degrees.

2 Grease an 8-inch flan dish or 9-inch pie pan if it does not have a nonstick surface. Place the pie crust in the pan and prick the base lightly with a fork in 8 to 10 places. Place a circle of waxed paper in the crust, and fill it with rice or pie weights. Bake the crust for about 10 minutes, but don't let it brown. Remove from the oven, and discard the waxed paper and rice or weights. Keep oven at 375 degrees.

3 Fry the bacon in a skillet over medium-low heat until browned and crisp. Drain thoroughly. Discard all but 1 tablespoon of the rendered fat. Add the butter or margarine. Sauté the shallots in the fat until they just begin to brown. Remove and drain, as with the bacon.

4 Beat the egg yolks and eggs with the cream and seasonings.

5 Place the bacon pieces and shallots evenly over the bottom of the shell. Ladle in the egg and cream mixture. Your work is now finished. Bake for about 25 minutes, or until the custard has puffed and browned. If a knife goes in and comes out clean, quiche is ready. Allow to cool slightly before removing from the pan. You can serve this hot or cold.

One-Dish Crab Dip

Makes 4 to 5 cups

Crab dips are always a hit as an hors d'oeuvre, and this one's a sure winner with both the guests and you, who will spend almost no time at all with its preparation.

3 8-ounce packages
  cream cheese
½ cup mayonnaise
2 teaspoons Dijon
  mustard
2 teaspoons
  confectioners' sugar
¼ cup sauterne wine
2 teaspoons onion juice
1 teaspoon Lawry's
  Seasoned Salt
3 8-ounce containers
  crabmeat, picked clean
  of shell

1 In a double boiler, melt the cream cheese. Stirring constantly, blend in the mayonnaise, mustard, confectioners' sugar, wine, onion juice, and seasoned salt.

2 Gently add the crabmeat, and continue cooking until the crab is warmed through.

3 Serve in a chafing dish, surrounded by crackers or toast points.

Keep A Couple Of Crusts

It's always a good idea to have a couple of pie crusts in the freezer for those times when a quick dessert or easy one-dish meal like quiche is needed.

Oysterette Munchies

Makes a lot, but they're so good, they'll probably be gone too soon

I've been asked for this recipe more than any other I've made for family and friends. These munchies take no effort to make, but they are the best crunchie-munchie you've ever made yourself. Watch out, though—once you start nibbling them, it's very difficult to stop. This is another of what I call "cousin" recipes: my father received it from a cousin, who received it from *her* cousin, who . . . you have a dozen of them, I'm sure. Now you have a great one that you can hand around.

¾ cup vegetable oil
1 teaspoon chopped dried dill
½ teaspoon garlic salt
1 teaspoon lemon pepper
1 package Hidden Valley Ranch Original Salad Dressing mix
2 7½-ounce boxes oyster crackers

1 In a medium bowl, whisk together the oil, dill, garlic salt, lemon pepper, and dressing mix.

2 Put the crackers in a large, flat pan such as a lasagne pan, and pour the herb mixture over them. With a spatula, turn and mix the crackers well, so that the herb mixture coats each cracker. Let the crackers stand at room temperature for at least 1 hour, but stir and turn them every 10 minutes or so.

3 Preheat the oven to 250 degrees. Put the uncovered pan in the warm oven and bake for 30 minutes. Again, stir several times so all sides of the crackers bake. Remove from the oven, cool, and store in a tight container until needed.

Sausage Balls

Makes 2 to 3 dozen balls

There's good news and bad news on these beauties. The good news is it will take you less than fifteen minutes to make a batch. The bad news is that they're so good they'll be gone in under that time. This is an old Bowersox favorite that is great fun to "fiddle with," as we like to say—you can add some heat if you'd like, in the form of Tabasco or other hot sauce; you can garlic them up (one of our favorites) by adding a few minced cloves of garlic; you can sweeten them a bit with a little brown sugar. Great fun for the kids to help make, too.

1 pound bulk sausage (hot or mild)
1 pound sharp cheddar cheese
3 cups Bisquick

1 Preheat the oven to 375 degrees.

2 Mix all ingredients in a large bowl. Shape into ¾- to 1-inch balls by rolling in the palms of the hands.

3 Bake on an ungreased cookie sheet for 15 minutes or so. Serve hot, or freeze for later use, reheating before serving.

Spinach Balls

Makes about 3 dozen balls

Like the Sausage Balls (page 53), these can be whipped together in no time. They, too, can be frozen if you'd like to get ahead on your plans for a gathering.

1 10-ounce package
frozen chopped spinach
1 cup herb-seasoned
stuffing mix
½ cup finely chopped
onion
3 eggs, beaten
¾ cup butter or
margarine, melted
¼ cup grated Parmesan
cheese
2 teaspoons garlic salt
¼ teaspoon dried thyme
2 teaspoons dried dill

1 Cook and drain the spinach, and place in a large bowl. Add the remaining ingredients and mix well. Chill for 30 minutes.

2 Preheat the oven to 350 degrees.

3 Roll mixture into bite-size balls between the palms of the hands. Bake for 20 minutes, then serve hot. Or make in advance and freeze them unbaked; thaw before baking.

Shrimp Cocktail with Ata Sauce

It's no secret that I love hot food. A good, spicy dip or sauce recipe is always welcome in my kitchen, and I love to serve them. This one makes a terrific dipping sauce for firm, cool shrimp, and it's not bad for cut vegetables, either. But "hot" is subjective. To me, hot is when it brings tears to your eyes and makes your nose run. You'll have to make your own judgment about this Ata Sauce, which is also known as African Red Dip. I've heated up the recipe a bit from the original, which I came across in *Betty Crocker's New International Cookbook.* You can tone it back down by dropping the Tabasco, halving the red pepper, and opting for a milder chili sauce. But personally, I'd go for it.

Ata Sauce

Mix the chili sauce and the Red Pepper Paste. Serve chilled with shrimp.

Red Pepper Paste

Put all the ingredients except the paprika in a blender or food processor and blend on high speed until smooth.

Heat the paprika in a 1-quart saucepan for 1 minute. Add the spice mixture gradually, stirring constantly until smooth. Cool before using in the Ata Sauce.

Makes enough sauce for 12 to 18 shrimp

1 cup hot chili sauce
2 tablespoons Red Pepper Paste
1 dozen cooked shrimp, peeled, deveined, and chilled

RED PEPPER PASTE
¼ cup dry red wine
1 ½ teaspoons ground red pepper
¾ teaspoon salt
¼ teaspoon ground ginger
⅛ teaspoon ground cardamom
⅛ teaspoon ground coriander
⅛ teaspoon ground nutmeg
⅛ teaspoon ground cloves
⅛ teaspoon ground cinnamon
⅛ teaspoon freshly ground black pepper
⅛ medium onion, chunked
2 garlic cloves
¼ cup paprika

Hot Broccoli Dip

Makes approximately
4 cups

¼ cup butter or
margarine
2 4-ounce cans
mushroom stems and
pieces, drained
½ cup chopped onion
2 10¾-ounce cans
condensed cream of
mushroom soup
2 5-ounce jars pasturized
sharp cheese spread
8 ounces sharp cheese,
cut into small cubes
18 to 20 ounces broccoli,
finely chopped
⅓ cup slivered almonds
½ teaspoon garlic
powder
1 teaspoon
Worcestershire sauce
3 or 4 drops Tabasco
sauce

This is a fine dip for a buffet table—colorful, enticing, and rich in flavor. It can be stored and reheated.

1 In a large skillet, melt the butter or margarine over medium-high heat. Add the mushrooms and onion, and sauté until the onion wilts, about 1 to 2 minutes. Add the soup and cheeses, and cook until the mixture becomes smooth and bubbly, stirring frequently.

2 Add the broccoli, almonds, garlic powder, Worcestershire sauce, and Tabasco. Simmer 8 minutes, stirring constantly.

3 Serve with tortilla chips or assorted crackers.

Pastas

Pasta is the perfect blank canvas. You can paint it with just about anything.

Whether you start with angel hair, linguine, fettuccine, or vermicelli, you'll have a willing recipient for your mixtures of color, texture, and taste.

Participant may be a better word for these pasta dishes, however; I'm inclined to think of the pasta in them as one element in the mix, rather than the "bottom" with a sauce on top. My wife's luxurious Primavera Parisi, for instance, is a garden of vegetables woven into the fettuccine, and the Pasta with Prosciutto and Olives is a wonderful coalescence of elements. I've also tried to balance the traditional, represented by a Spaghetti Carbonara, with the cross-cultural, as with the Pasta with Korean Sesame Sauce. And then there's the seductive Angel Hair with Crab—so easy a temptation to succumb to.

I suggest making the pasta fresh, either by hand or by machine. There really is no comparison in the final product, and it cooks in only 2 to 3 minutes.

Primavera Parisi

Makes 4 to 6 servings

QVC viewers have often heard me speak of my wife, Toni. The fact of the matter is, our viewers watched as Toni and I became engaged, got married, and two years later, had our daughter, Taylor. She's almost as familiar to them as I am. QVC is one large family, anyway, so it doesn't seem odd to me in the least when a caller asks how Toni is.

Unfortunately, the viewers have *not* had the distinct pleasure of sitting down to one of Toni's wonderful creations. Though I do a great deal of cooking at home, I am always more than willing to pass the apron to her. Half Italian and half Polish, she's a creative cook who has a knack for coming up with dishes whose flavors stick to your memory—just hearing the name conjures up the taste. Primavera Parisi (her maiden name) is one such dish, and has become one of my favorites. It's one of those dishes you want to keep eating until you bust, the flavors are so rich and satisfying. I particularly love it cold the next day, though there are seldom any leftovers. There are few ingredients, and you will find yourself sitting down to enjoy it very soon after beginning to cook it—it's that quick and easy.

2 cups broccoli flowerettes
2 cups cauliflower flowerettes
2 cups julienned carrots, 2 inches long and ¼ inch square
12 ounces fettuccine noodles
½ cup softened butter or margarine
1 cup heavy cream, at room temperature
¾ cup grated Parmesan cheese
Salt and pepper to taste
2 tablespoons chopped fresh parsley

1 In a large saucepan or Dutch oven, steam the vegetables until crisp-tender, and still colorful. Keep warm.

2 Cook the fettuccine according to package instructions, or for fresh-made, for 3 minutes in slightly salted boiling water. Drain the noodles thoroughly just before using, but keep hot.

3 In a large serving bowl, mix the noodles, butter or margarine, cream, and cheese. Add the steamed vegetables and toss again. Season with salt and pepper.

4 Sprinkle individual servings with a little parsley and serve immediately. Have Parmesan cheese on the table if you should desire a bit more.

Asian Primavera

Makes 2 servings

Add a tangy oriental flavor to the traditional pasta primavera.

1 In a small bowl, stir together the broth, soy sauce, sugar, and vinegar. Set aside.

3/4 cup chicken broth
1 tablespoon soy sauce
1/2 tablespoon sugar
1/2 tablespoon white wine vinegar
2 tablespoons sesame seeds
2 tablespoons vegetable oil
2 garlic cloves, minced
1 tablespoon minced fresh ginger
2 ounces fresh white mushrooms or 3 large shiitake mushrooms, thinly sliced
1 cup thinly sliced bok choy
4 ounces snowpeas
2 tablespoons dry sherry
2 ounces ham, thinly sliced and julienned
8 ounces angel hair pasta

2 In a wide frying pan or wok over medium-high heat, toast the sesame seeds until golden, about 2 to 3 minutes. Pour seeds into bowl and reserve.

3 Return the pan to the heat, and warm the oil. Add the garlic and ginger and cook, stirring, until wilted. Add the mushrooms, bok choy, snowpeas, and sherry. Cook until the snowpeas are bright green. Pour in the broth mixture and bring to a boil. Add the ham and cook briefly. Remove from heat and keep warm.

4 While vegetables are being prepared, cook the pasta in boiling water with a pinch of salt.

5 Add the drained pasta to the vegetables and mix lightly. Divide the pasta between 2 plates and sprinkle with the sesame seeds.

Fresh Pasta

Whenever possible, make your own pasta, whether it be by the old hand-crank method or with one of the many new automatic machines. The difference in flavor and texture is enormous, and the pasta cooks in one-third the time.

Angel Hair with Crab

I've never quite understood settling for a bottled sauce over pasta, no matter how many goodies they say they can cram into the jar. It doesn't take much more time to do something out of the ordinary, and the rewards for your efforts can sometimes be significant. Take this crab sauce, for instance, developed by the Sunset kitchens for their *Italian Cook Book*. A few minutes for preparation of ingredients, a few more for cooking, and you have something fresh and interesting to the eye and palate. This is a marvelous appetizer as well, if you're looking for a distinctive opener for a dinner party.

8 ounces angel hair pasta
2 tablespoons butter or margarine
¼ cup olive oil (or vegetable oil, if you prefer a lighter flavor)
½ cup sliced green onions (with tops)
2 garlic cloves, minced
2 medium tomatoes, peeled, seeded, and chopped
¼ cup dry white wine
1 tablespoon lemon juice
½ pound cooked crabmeat, cleaned and flaked
¼ cup chopped fresh parsley
Salt and pepper to taste
Lemon wedges (as garnish)

1 Cook the pasta as instructed, drain well, and place on a warm platter.

2 While pasta is cooking, place the butter or margarine and the oil in a wide frying pan over medium-high heat. When the butter is melted, add the green onions, garlic, tomatoes, and wine. Cook, stirring until the mixture boils. Reduce heat to achieve a gentle simmer. Simmer 2 minutes.

3 Mix in the lemon juice, crab, and parsley. Cook just until the crab is heated through. Season with salt and pepper and stir.

4 Carefully pour the sauce over the pasta. Lift and mix the pasta and sauce gently. Serve with lemon wedges.

To Quickly Remove a Tomato Skin

A tomato's skin can be quickly and easily removed without too much trouble. Simply bring a saucepan of water to a boil, then gently lower the tomato into it. As soon as the water returns to a boil, remove the tomato. The skin can then be easily pulled away.

Pasta with Prosciutto and Olives

This is another pasta dish that takes very little time to prepare, but offers that "I slaved most of the day to make this for you" look and taste. It's particularly suited to angel hair or linguine, but I've made it with fettuccine with excellent results as well. This is another recipe from the Italian side of the family.

8 ounces pasta (fettuccine, linguine, angel hair)

1 Cook pasta until al dente (slightly firm, not mushy), and place in a warm bowl.

2 ounces prosciutto, thinly sliced and cut into ¼-inch strips
¼ cup olive oil
½ cup thinly sliced green onions (including tops)
1 3-ounce jar pimiento-stuffed green olives, drained
1 cup cherry tomatoes, halved
Grated Parmesan cheese

2 While the pasta is cooking, place the prosciutto and oil over medium-high heat in a wide frying pan. Cook until the prosciutto is slightly brown, stirring frequently to turn the prosciutto. Add the green onions and continue cooking until they are wilted. Add the olives and tomatoes next, and cook, stirring often, until warmed, but still firm.

3 Pour the sauce over the pasta in a large saucepan or Dutch oven, toss well, and warm. Serve with grated Parmesan on the table.

Pasta with Korean Sesame Sauce

Makes 4 to 6 servings

8 to 10 ounces pasta
(fettuccine, spaghetti,
angel hair)
1 tablespoon oriental
sesame oil
3 tablespoons distilled
white vinegar
2 tablespoons hot bean
paste
2 tablespoons soy sauce
3 tablespoons sliced
green onions
2 garlic cloves, minced
1 teaspoon sugar
1 teaspoon pepper
2 teaspoons finely grated
fresh ginger
2 tablespoons sesame
seeds
1 medium cucumber,
thinly sliced
(as garnish)

I always know when a recipe is a winner on *In the Kitchen with Bob*. I can gauge its success in two ways. The first is by the number of requests I get for the recipe. Most recipes generate 1,500 to 2,500 requests, a real winner hits about 4,000 minimum.

The second gauge is the number of QVC product coordinators (PCs) that swarm around the dish once it leaves the set. Product coordinators are the young folks who keep track of all the products for each show, and place them on the set when it's time to present them. It's an entry-level position at QVC, and most of the PCs are fresh out of college, so any chance they have to grab a free meal, they take it. But they're picky eaters, and I've learned that there's a direct correlation between a good recipe and the number of PCs sticking a fork into the dish.

Pasta with Korean Sesame Sauce is one of the all-time winners. I still have PCs ask me when and if I plan to make it again. It's based on a recipe in the *Low Cholesterol Cookbook*, with a few changes here and there. Simple and quick, its exotic oriental sensibilities are sure to please those looking for something unusual.

1 In a bowl, combine the sesame oil, vinegar, bean paste, soy sauce, green onions, garlic, sugar, pepper, and ginger. Set aside.

2 In a large frying pan over medium heat, toast the sesame seeds until golden, about 2 to 3 minutes. You may find that shaking the pan occasionally helps with even toasting.

3 Cook the pasta in lightly salted boiling water until al dente. Drain the pasta and add to the frying pan. Then add the vinegar mixture and toss the pasta well. Serve with cucumber garnish.

Spaghetti Carbonara

Makes 6 servings

A classic, and one of my favorite pasta dishes, for both the wonderful mix of Italian flavors and the ease of preparation. It's also a great dish to experiment with, in that you can exchange the prosciutto for ground beef, if you'd like, or lean bacon for mild Italian sausages. This version is a mix of several that I've come across, most prominently Craig Claiborne's.

¼ **pound lean bacon**
2 **medium onions, finely chopped**
3 **tablespoons extra-virgin olive oil**
Salt and freshly ground pepper
5 **tablespoons chopped fresh parsley**
½ **cup chopped prosciutto (or ¾ pound lean ground beef, ¼ teaspoon fennel seeds, 1 garlic clove, minced)**
½ **pound Fontina cheese, diced**
1 **pound spaghetti**
4 **eggs, beaten**
Grated Parmesan cheese

1 Cut the bacon into pieces approximately 1 inch square, and cook in a wide frying pan until crisp, then drain on paper towels and set aside.

2 In a large saucepan over medium-high heat, sauté the onions in the olive oil until wilted. Add the salt, pepper, parsley, prosciutto or beef, garlic, and fennel seeds, bacon, and Fontina. Cover and simmer for 5 minutes.

3 Meanwhile, cook the pasta until al dente in boiling water with a little salt. Drain the pasta when done, and place in a large serving bowl. Add the eggs and toss well to cover the pasta as much as possible (the egg helps to hold the other ingredients evenly on the pasta).

4 Add the sauce and toss again, then serve immediately with Parmesan cheese on the table.

Make Ahead

Try to choose one evening a week to do "make-ahead" cooking. Make a couple of sauces that can be frozen and then easily thawed for quick use another night. Or create two or three pasta dishes, such as lasagne or ravioli, that will freeze well and can be defrosted as they bake in the oven or boil in the pot.

Linguine with a Mushroom Sauce

Makes 6 servings

A friend once said to me during a dinner party that he thought mushrooms were an acquired taste, much as Scotch is: you either like them or you don't. He didn't. Another friend at the table thought it was a moot point—mushrooms *had* no taste, as far as he was concerned. To both I offer this dish, and I hope they'll take the few minutes necessary to see how intriguing and flavorful mushrooms can be.

8 ounces linguine
2 tablespoons olive oil
3 to 4 ounces mushrooms, thinly sliced
1 small onion, chopped
2 garlic cloves, finely chopped
1 cup whipping (heavy) cream
½ teaspoon salt
¼ teaspoon coarsely ground pepper

1 Cook the linguine until al dente, drain, and keep warm in a heated bowl.

2 While pasta is cooking, heat the oil in a large skillet over medium-high heat. Add the mushrooms, onion, and garlic and cook until onion is tender, about 1 to 2 minutes. Add the cream and salt and heat to boiling, stirring often. Reduce heat and simmer uncovered for 5 minutes or until slightly thickened.

3 Pour the sauce over the drained linguine and toss until well coated. Serve with the pepper on the side.

Ingredient Temperature

Have all your ingredients at room temperature if you can. This way, everything starts at the same point, and adding a cooler ingredient will not slow the cooking process of a dish.

Mushroom Broccoli Stroganoff

Makes 8 servings

Though this tasty vegetable casserole takes thirty minutes to bake, you'll have it in the oven in just a few minutes. It's a neat twist on the traditional beef dish, and makes an excellent side dish as well as a vegetable entree. The basic recipe is another winner created by the Sunset kitchens, but I've added a few touches I thought enhanced the flavors a bit.

2 tablespoons butter or
   margarine
1 large onion, chopped
½ pound mushrooms,
   sliced
2 tablespoons lemon
   juice
½ teaspoon salt
½ teaspoon dried basil
1 cup sour cream
¼ cup dry white wine
⅛ teaspoon ground
   nutmeg
1 cup shredded Monterey
   Jack cheese
1 cup shredded cheddar
   cheese
1½ pounds broccoli
1 12-ounce package
   spinach noodles
⅓ cup chopped walnuts

1 Preheat the oven to 350 degrees.

2 Melt the butter or margarine in a wide frying pan over medium heat. Add the onion and mushrooms and cook until wilted, about 1 to 2 minutes. Remove the pan from the heat and stir in the lemon juice, salt, basil, sour cream, white wine, and nutmeg. Mix in ½ cup each of the two cheeses. Set aside.

3 Cut the broccoli into small flowerettes, and chunk-dice the stems. Steam the broccoli until just crisp-tender and bright green, about 5 minutes.

4 While the broccoli is steaming, cook the noodles in a pot of boiling, salted water. Time them so they are al dente just as the broccoli is finished. Drain thoroughly.

5 In a large bowl, combine the sour cream mixture, the broccoli, and the noodles. Toss well. Turn into a shallow 3-quart baking dish, and bake for 25 minutes.

6 Sprinkle the remaining cheese and the walnuts on top of the casserole and bake for another 5 minutes. Serve hot with cheeses bubbling on top.

Fish and Shellfish

It's rather well known that I adore seafood. First and last, I'd rather cook, serve, and enjoy fish or shellfish than anything else. Give me the creamy Crab Newburg Muffins for breakfast, the delicate Poisson Véronique for midday, and the bright, savory Swordfish with Tarragon, Garlic, and Shallots for the evening meal, and I'll call that a good day.

I tend to favor poaching fish over pan-frying, baking, or broiling because it is an extremely efficient method of preparing the dish. Whether it be steak or fillet, I think you'll spend less time poaching. But more than that, poaching allows you to quickly infuse the flesh of the fish with nuance or accent, be it just a subtle touch or a rich involvement of flavor. Try the subtleness of a little white wine and thyme in the Flounder Florentine (not to mention the beauty of the rolled fillets), or the spicy heat of the African Poached Fish, or the light, clean finish of Fish Steaks with Green Salsa. All are poached, but none of them is remotely alike.

On the shellfish side, my fondness for

scallops is represented by the Scallop and Vegetable Pesto Sauté, with its nutty, garlic overtones, and for the crab lovers, there's the luxurious Crab Baked with Port Wine casserole. Patrice Boely's Prawns Early Morning may just be my all-time favorite shrimp dish. And if you can't make up your mind which seafood to try, opt for the Seafood Paella—there's a little bit of everything in that.

Fish Steaks
with Green Salsa

Makes 2 servings

Salsa has always been one of my favorite taste sensations. When done well, it's one of the few mixtures of ingredients that allows itself to be experienced both as a whole and through each of its constituent parts.

Most of us have tried the traditional red salsas, which can be mild or hot, and are usually served with chips or vegetables as a finger food. But salsas, as mixtures, can really be anything you wish them to be. They are usually onion based, but above that, do as you wish. The salsa used in this recipe is based in green herbs and vegetables—cilantro, parsley, and jalapeños. It's a perfect topping for any fish, especially swordfish, red snapper, or tuna.

GREEN SALSA
1 small onion, finely chopped
1 cup chopped fresh cilantro
½ cup chopped fresh parsley
½ cup olive oil
½ cup lime juice
3 tablespoons distilled white vinegar
3 garlic cloves, minced
1 jalapeño pepper, seeded and minced

2 tablespoons lemon juice
1 small dried hot chili pepper
2 tablespoons chopped fresh cilantro
1 14½-ounce can chicken broth
1 pound fish steaks (red snapper, tuna, swordfish), cut in half
2 cups shredded lettuce
¾ cup sour cream
Lime wedges (as garnish)

1 Prepare the green salsa by combining all the ingredients in a small saucepan. Place on medium-low heat and keep warm while preparing the fish.

2 In a large, shallow frying pan, combine the lemon juice, chili pepper, cilantro, and broth. Bring to a boil over high heat, then reduce heat to a simmer. Arrange the fish in the broth, and cover. Simmer until the fish flakes easily.

3 Place about 1 cup of the shredded lettuce in the center of each serving plate. Rest the fish on top of the lettuce. Top the fish with a dollop of the sour cream, and then spoon the salsa over the sour cream and fish. Serve immediately with lime wedges.

Seafood Paella

Makes 6 to 8 servings

2 tablespoons olive oil
3 garlic cloves, thinly
   sliced
½ cup coarsely chopped
   onion
¾ cup cored and cubed
   unpeeled tomatoes
1 or 2 Spanish sausages,
   cut into ¼-inch slices
1 cup shrimp, shelled
   and deveined
2 tablespoons drained
   capers
¼ cup tomato paste
6 cherrystone clams
¾ cup bay scallops
½ cup shucked oysters
4 cups chicken broth,
   heated
1 bay leaf
½ teaspoon dried
   oregano
1 ¼ cups quick-cooking
   long-grain rice
Tabasco sauce to taste
3 cups shredded cooked
   boneless chicken
Spanish olives stuffed
   with pimientos
   (as garnish)
Hard-boiled eggs
   (as garnish)

*P*aella, in the original French, means "small pan." I suppose that the original paellas could have evolved from peasants tossing odds and ends of meats and vegetables into such a pan, and indeed, a good modern-day paella is a rich mixture of ingredients. But today we can make them as big as we want to.

Almost every cook who loves seafood has a personal recipe for a paella, each one weighted toward a favorite seafood. The original version offered here came from Craig Claiborne, and is one of the better-balanced I've tried. I've altered it slightly to meet my tastes and needs. It cooks up quickly, so you don't have to wait too long for that special spiciness that is paella.

1 Heat the oil in a paella pan or wide, deep skillet. When hot, add the garlic. Just as the garlic begins to turn brown, remove and discard it.

2 Add the onion and the tomatoes and cook briefly. Add the sausages and cook for another 5 minutes. Add the shrimp and cook until they turn coral, about 3 minutes. Then add the capers and tomato paste, stirring to blend thoroughly. Add the clams, scallops, and oysters. Cook for another 2 minutes, add 3 cups of the hot chicken broth, the bay leaf, and the oregano.

3 Gradually sprinkle the rice into the pan, and stir constantly. Add the Tabasco. Simmer for about 5 minutes, stirring frequently. Add the last 1 cup of the heated broth.

4 Add the chicken, and stir to distribute it throughout the pan. Cook just long enough to heat the chicken through and until the rice is tender. Remove the bay leaf. Garnish with Spanish olives and wedges of hard-boiled eggs.

Swordfish in a Tomato-Olive Sauce

Makes 2 servings

Swordfish is an easy fish to fall in love with. Grilled, broiled, poached, steamed—it doesn't really matter how you prepare it   it works with you, quickly, and with little cajoling. The flesh is firmer than most fish, and when done, has a wonderful creamy whiteness that makes a superb neutral palette for a colorful sauce. This tomato-olive sauce is just that—a beautiful mix of reds and greens. The Sunset kitchens, who developed the sauce, call it "confetti"; you'll call it delicious.

TOMATO-OLIVE SAUCE
- 1½ medium tomatoes, seeded and finely chopped
- ¾ cup pimiento-stuffed olives
- 3 tablespoons drained capers
- 5 tablespoons sliced green onions (including tops)
- 5 tablespoons lime juice
- 4 tablespoons olive oil

- 2 swordfish steaks, about 7 ounces each, 1 inch thick
- 1 tablespoon olive oil
- ½ cup dry white wine
- Lime wedges

1 Prepare the tomato-olive sauce by combining all ingredients in a bowl. Set aside.

2 Rinse the fish, pat it dry, and then brush both sides with the olive oil. Place the steaks in a wide frying pan over medium-high heat. Just as you hear the oil starting to sizzle a bit under the fish, add the wine. Lower the heat so you achieve a low simmer, then cover and poach until the fish is just opaque and flakes slightly at the touch of a fork, about 5 to 7 minutes.

3 Add the tomato-olive sauce to the wine around the fish (add a bit more wine if it has evaporated). Make sure you don't overcook the sauce, as you want the tomatoes firm. Just cook it long enough to warm it thoroughly.

4 Place the fish on individual serving plates, topped with equal parts of the sauce. Serve with lime wedges.

Red Snapper in an Orange-Lime Sauce

Makes 4 servings

Few recipes have the ability to make your mouth water just by having read the name. Doesn't this one sound marvelous? You can almost taste the tanginess of the citrus. Very often seafood sauces get a little too heavy, with lots of cream and butter, but this is a refreshing alternative. I've found it particularly pleasing on hot summer nights, when heaviness is completely wrong and quick cooking times are an absolute must.

2 tablespoons olive oil
4 red snapper steaks or fillets, about 8 ounces each
Salt and pepper to taste
8 bay leaves
1 cup virgin olive oil
3 oranges, peeled and divided into sections
5 limes, peeled and divided into sections
1 tablespoon butter or margarine
1 16-ounce can whole small white potatoes
½ teaspoon chopped fresh parsley

1 In a large frying pan or skillet, put 1 tablespoon of the olive oil and heat over medium to medium-high heat. Place the fish steaks in the pan, brush with olive oil, and flip over, then brush again. Season with salt and pepper, cover, and cook, turning once or twice until fish flakes easily with a fork, about 5 minutes.

2 While the fish is cooking, combine the remaining olive oil, salt and pepper, and the orange and lime sections in a saucepan over medium heat. Heat the sauce until smooth, but don't allow it to boil—you don't want to break down the citrus sections.

3 In a second saucepan, combine the butter or margarine, potatoes, and parsley. Cook until heated thoroughly.

4 Place each portion of fish on an individual plate, with a serving of parsley potatoes. Serve immediately. Pour the sauce into a gravy bowl or sauceboat, and place on table for passing.

Let the Market Save You Time

Try to buy your fish and meats at a market where they'll cut or fillet the items to your specific needs. It will save you time in preparation at home.

Flounder Florentine

Makes 4 servings

One of the easiest but most impressive fish entrees you can make. It allows you to bring the lowly flounder into a dressier role. The sauce is formed by your poaching liquid, which virtually eliminates a whole step from the cooking process. The flounder rolls can be made a few hours in advance, saving you even more time for your guests.

4 flounder fillets, 6 inches long by 3 or 4 inches wide
12 ounces fresh spinach
4 tablespoons lemon juice
2 tablespoons butter or margarine
3 tablespoons finely chopped Bermuda onion
1 teaspoon chopped dried thyme
¾ cup dry white wine
Salt and pepper to taste
4 thyme sprigs (as garnish)
Lemon wedges (as garnish)

1 Wash the flounder fillets, pat them dry, and lay them out flat on your preparation surface.

2 Wash the spinach thoroughly, and remove any overly long and stringy stems. Chop the leaves finely without mincing them.

3 Spread a layer of the chopped spinach along the length and width of each fillet. Sprinkle 1 tablespoon of lemon juice over each. Then roll the fillets from the narrow end to the wider end, and secure the roll with 2 or 3 toothpicks. (You'll want to use the natural wood toothpicks, as the dye for the colored ones will leach into the fish.) Set aside.

4 In a large skillet that has a lid, melt the butter or margarine over medium-high heat. Add the onion and sauté until translucent, about 1 to 2 minutes. Add the thyme and stir, then add the wine.

5 Place the flounder rolls in the skillet, and baste with the wine and onion sauce. Cover and poach for 5 to 8 minutes. If the liquid gets low, add a bit more wine a tablespoon at a time, so as not to cool the fish. Add salt and pepper to taste, and serve hot with a thyme sprig over the roll and lemon wedges on the side.

Salsa Cod

A freshly made salsa brings a bright color and invigorating flavor to this dish. Since fresh cod is an almost neutral fish as regards flavor, the spices and nuances of your salsa will stand out. If you're in a hurry, you can even speed up an already fast preparation by simply using any ready-made salsa.

SALSA

1 ½ cups finely chopped tomatoes
½ cup finely chopped onion
3 garlic cloves, minced
1 jalapeño pepper, finely chopped (add more if you like heat)
1 tablespoon lemon juice
1 teaspoon vegetable oil
1 ½ teaspoons chopped fresh oregano or ½ teaspoon dried
1 ½ teaspoons chopped fresh cilantro

4 cod fillets, 7 to 8 ounces each
1 garlic clove, minced
1 tablespoon butter or margarine
⅔ cup dry white wine
Fresh lime wedges (as garnish)

1 Prepare the salsa by combining all the ingredients in a medium saucepan over medium-low heat. Keep warm and stir frequently.

2 Put the garlic and margarine in a large skillet or frying pan over medium heat. When the garlic just begins to brown, add the wine. Gently lay the fish fillets in the pan; cover, and poach until fish flakes at the touch of a fork, about 5 minutes.

3 Serve immediately with warm salsa ladled over the fish, with 2 or 3 lime wedges on the side.

Poisson Véronique
Fish with Grapes

Makes 4 servings

This is a dish I adapted for crepes in my restaurant, The Crepe Chalet. It became one of the most requested items on the menu. The grapes add a sweetness to the sauce not achievable by adding mere sugar—it's that cool, tangy sweetness that you can only get from fresh, green grapes. Though there are a number of steps to the process, each step takes very little time.

2 pounds fish fillets (haddock, scrod, or cod)
1½ teaspoons salt
¼ teaspoon pepper
¾ cup dry white wine
1 cup water
2 tablespoons finely chopped shallots
1 tablespoon lemon juice
8 ounces green seedless grapes, each grape halved
4 tablespoons butter or margarine
2 tablespoons flour
½ cup whipping (heavy) cream
Whole green grapes (as garnish)

1 Wash the fish and pat it dry. Sprinkle it with salt and pepper. Set aside momentarily.

2 In a 10- or 12-inch skillet over medium-high heat, combine the wine, water, shallots, and lemon juice. Fold the fish in half across its width, and place in the skillet; or if using smaller fillets, lay them side by side. Bring to a boil, then reduce the heat, cover, and poach 3 to 4 minutes. Remove the fish and place it in a heated warming dish with a cover. Retain the liquids in the skillet.

3 Add the grapes to the skillet and return to a boil, about 1 minute, no longer. Remove the grapes and add them to the warming dish with the fish, and pour the liquid into a measuring cup.

4 Heat 2 tablespoons of the butter or margarine in the skillet and stir in the flour, making a smooth roux. Add the grape liquid, and the cream. Heat to a boil once again, then reduce heat and stir in the other 2 tablespoons of butter or margarine. Stir sauce to smoothness.

5 At this point you can do one of two services: Serve the fish on large platter, topped with the Véronique sauce; or spoon the sauce over the fish in the warming dish and place it under a broiler for 1 to 2 minutes until the sauce is slightly glazed. Serve with grapes as a garnish.

Swordfish with Tarragon, Garlic, and Shallots

Makes 4 servings

Swordfish and tarragon. Two loves. I've been working on this one for a number of years, but have never made it on *In the Kitchen with Bob.* The recipe began as swordfish simply poached in white wine. But of course, I couldn't leave well enough alone, so it has evolved. First I added the garlic, then the shallots. I was content with that for a while, when my wife, Toni, felt it could use some color, so in came the tomatoes.

Then I fell in love with tarragon. And that sealed it. It really doesn't take all that much time to prepare—it cooks faster than it preps, actually—and I've had great success with the dish at a number of private dinner parties. I'm sure you will, too.

3 tablespoons margarine
**3 or 4 garlic cloves,
  finely chopped**
**2 large shallots, finely
  chopped**
1 cup dry white wine
**1 teaspoon chopped
  dried tarragon**
**4 medium swordfish
  steaks, about 8 ounces
  each, trimmed into
  rough ovals**
**2 large, firm tomatoes,
  chunked**
Salt and pepper to taste

1 In a large skillet with a lid, melt the margarine over medium heat. Add the garlic and shallots. When they are wilted and just beginning to brown, in about 2 to 3 minutes, add the wine and tarragon and stir to blend well. Bring the mixture to a simmer.

2 Wash the swordfish steaks and place them in the skillet. Baste once or twice with the liquid, then cover and poach for about 5 minutes. If the steaks are more than 1 inch thick, they should be turned at about 3 minutes.

3 Just as the fish is approaching an easy flaking at the prod of a fork, add the tomatoes. Place them around the swordfish, not on it. If the liquid is reducing away, add a little more wine by the tablespoonful until bottom is again covered. You won't need much, as the tomatoes will be giving up some water when they cook. Add salt and pepper as desired.

4 To serve, place each steak on an individual serving plate and spoon some of the sauce over it. There should be enough to cover all steaks well. Serve immediately.

Thon à la Provençale
Tuna Provençale

Makes 4 servings

The French province of Provence lies along the Mediterranean Sea in eastern France. Its cuisine is one of olives and olive oil, tomatoes, garlic, herbs, and, of course, seafood. It was here that the first true bouillabaisse was created. Tuna is an easy catch for Mediterranean fishermen, and so will be found on any inn's menu. This is a simple baked dish, and one that you'll find yourself making more than once because of its simplicity and its mix of flavors Provençale.

4 7-ounce tuna steaks, or 4 rounds of canned tuna (6⅛ ounces each), unbroken
Juice of ½ lemon
Salt and pepper to taste
8 anchovy fillets
1 tablespoon olive oil
1 medium onion, chopped
4 ripe tomatoes, peeled and chopped
1 garlic clove, crushed
¾ cup dry white wine

BOUQUET GARNI
1 bay leaf
1 teaspoon chopped dried thyme
1 teaspoon chopped dried parsley
1 teaspoon chopped dried basil
1 teaspoon chopped dried tarragon
1 teaspoon chopped dried chives

Lemon wedges (as garnish)

1 Preheat the oven to 350 degrees.

2 Place the tuna steaks or rounds in an oven baking dish or casserole dish. Sprinkle the lemon juice over them, along with salt and pepper. Lay 2 anchovy fillets on each steak or round in an X. Set aside.

3 In a saucepan over medium-high heat, combine the oil and onion. Cook until the onion wilts, about 1 to 2 minutes, then add the tomatoes, garlic, wine, and bouquet garni. Boil rapidly, uncovered, until reduced and thickened, about 3 to 5 minutes. Your work is now done.

4 Pour the sauce over the tuna, cover, and bake for 10 to 12 minutes. Remove the bouquet garni before serving. Garnish with lemon wedges.

Note: A bouquet garni is a small sachet of herbs that is used to infuse a dish with the flavors of the herbs without adding them directly to the recipe. The herbs can be mixed and wrapped in a piece of cheesecloth or a handkerchief, or placed in a stainless teaball.

Sole with a Pistachio Butter Sauce

Makes 4 servings

1 ½ pounds thin sole or flounder fillets
Flour
⅓ cup margarine or butter
2 tablespoons vegetable oil
¼ cup thinly sliced green onions (with tops)
½ cup dry vermouth
½ cup chicken broth
⅓ cup salted or unsalted roasted pistachios, shelled and coarsely chopped
Lemon wedges (as garnish)
Parsley sprigs (as garnish)

Pistachios add a marvelous nutty flavor to this dish that becomes truly distinctive when blended with the vermouth. This recipe, originally found in Sunset's *Quick & Easy Cook Book,* is one of the most requested on *In the Kitchen with Bob.*

1 Rinse the fish and dust with the flour; shake off the excess. Set aside.

2 Melt 1 tablespoon of the margarine in 1 tablespoon of the oil in a wide frying pan over medium-high heat. Add the fish. Cook, turning once, until the fish is just opaque, but still moist, about 3 to 5 minutes. Remove the fish and transfer to a warm platter.

3 To the skillet, add the green onions, vermouth, and broth. Bring to a boil, then reduce to a vigorous simmer until sauce is reduced by half. Reduce the heat again and add ¼ cup of margarine all at once. Stir constantly until the margarine is completely blended into sauce. Stir in the pistachios and cook until just warm.

4 Divide the fish among the individual serving plates, and spoon the pistachio sauce over each. Serve with lemon wedges and parsley.

Watch Your Thickness

One way to speed cooking time with fish is to cut your fish fillets no thicker than ½ inch and your fish steaks no thicker than ¾ to 1 inch.

African Poached Fish

Known in Kenya as *mtuzi wa samaki,* this dish has at its soul the spicy nature of most African cooking. The cuisine uses peppers, garlic, and herbs in ways that have since found their way into my everyday cooking. I would never have become interested in African cuisine had it not been for *Betty Crocker's New International Cookbook.* It has several great African recipes, all of which are easy and quick to prepare, and a joy to consume.

2 tablespoons vege-
  table oil
1 large onion, sliced
2 garlic cloves, chopped
2 jalapeño peppers,
  seeded and chopped
1 pound whole tomatoes,
  chopped
2 tablespoons vinegar
1 ¼ teaspoons ground
  cumin
¾ teaspoon ground
  coriander
½ teaspoon salt
4 halibut steaks or fillets,
  about 7 ounces each
Chopped fresh cilantro
  (optional)

1 In a 10-inch skillet or larger, heat the oil over medium heat. Add the onion, garlic, and jalapeño peppers, and sauté until the onion is tender, about 1 to 2 minutes. Reduce the heat and stir in all remaining ingredients except the fish. Cook uncovered over low heat, stirring occasionally, for 5 minutes.

2 Gently nestle the fish steaks or fillets into the skillet, sliding them in among the tomatoes and herbs. Bring the mixture to a low simmer and cover. Baste the fish frequently with the liquid in the skillet.

3 When the fish flakes easily, serve in the center of a plate with a ladle or two of the tomato mixture around it. Sprinkle with a pinch of cilantro, if desired.

Bermudian Poached Fish

Makes 4 servings

If you're interested in gaining some insights into new ways to prepare fish, I suggest you spend a week or two on Bermuda. Not only do they have more fin fish offerings than I've seen anywhere, they are wonderfully creative in the seasonings they use.

Every time I vacation on Bermuda, I bring back new ideas. This recipe came from one such trip. We spent most of the dining evening working out just exactly what was in the dish, and were finally treated to the approximate measures by the waiter, whose brother was the chef. I've adapted it a bit for quick preparation, but the dish remains the same.

2 tablespoons olive oil
1 shallot or pungent onion, finely chopped
1 garlic clove, minced
1 ½ cups dry white wine
1 teaspoon chopped dried basil
1 ½ pounds fish fillets (we had grouper, but almost any white-fleshed fish will do)
1 medium carrot, julienned
1 medium potato, julienned
1 Bermuda onion, cut into ¼-inch slices, halved
½ red bell pepper, julienned
½ green bell pepper, julienned
½ yellow bell pepper, julienned
Salt and pepper to taste
3 cups cooked rice
Lemon wedges (as garnish)

1 Heat the oil in a poaching pan or deep, wide skillet over medium-high heat. Add the shallot or onion and the garlic and sauté until they are wilted, about 1 to 2 minutes. Add the wine and ½ teaspoon of the basil. Heat to a low simmer.

2 Wash the fish and pat it dry. Place the fillet in the wine and vegetables, criss-crossing the julienned strips of pepper and carrot in an X pattern over the length of the fillet. Sprinkle the fish with the other ½ teaspoon of basil, and the salt and pepper. Frequently spoon the liquid over the fish. Cover and simmer for about 5 minutes. Serve over rice, with lemon wedges as garnish.

Think ''Small''

Keep the size of your ingredients on the small side. For instance, mince your garlic, onions, and herbs. When the recipe calls for a julienned vegetable, make it longer and thinner. For a ''chop,'' make the pieces about ¼ inch square, or a cube ¼ inch on a side. The ingredients will cook much faster.

Crab Baked
with Port Wine

Makes 4 servings

A great casserole. It literally takes minutes to prepare, and only twenty minutes to bake to perfection. The succulent, sweet crabmeat is surrounded with one of Spain's greatest achievements—Port wine—and the golden crust that tops it all is inviting evidence of the warm pleasure crab lovers will find within. A little extra heat is added by some red pepper sauce. It makes a marvelous dip, served with toast points, or an irresistible first course.

½ **cup mayonnaise**
½ **cup whipping (heavy) cream**
6 tablespoons Port wine
2 tablespoons drained capers
2 tablespoons diced pimientos
1 teaspoon dry mustard
1 teaspoon salt
2 green onions, sliced (with tops)
12 drops red pepper sauce
2 pounds lump crabmeat, picked clean
4 tablespoons dry bread crumbs
2 teaspoons butter or margarine
Chopped parsley
Lemon wedges (as garnish)

1 Preheat the oven to 375 degrees.

2 In a medium bowl, mix the mayonnaise, cream, wine, capers, pimientos, mustard, salt, green onions, and pepper sauce. Gently stir in the crabmeat, being careful not to break it up too much. (You want some large chunks in there for the die-hard crab lovers!) Pour the mixture into a shallow casserole dish.

3 Mix the bread crumbs and margarine together in a small bowl, until the consistency is that of crumb topping. Sprinkle over the top of the casserole.

4 Bake until bubbly and the crumb topping is golden brown, no more than 20 minutes. Sprinkle with parsley and serve with lemon wedges.

Crab Newburg Muffins

Makes 6 servings

I remember my father making these for us every summer when we would spend two weeks in Wildwood Crest on the New Jersey shore. He made them only then, never at home. I suppose part of his thinking was that he wasn't going to keep us kids inside for very long, so he had to whip up something quickly, or we'd be out the door and gone. The other part had to be his love of crabs, and the fact that fresh-caught crabs were readily available any time of the day or night at the Jersey shore. If you're at all like my dad—a crab lover in a hurry—you'll appreciate his Newburg Muffins recipe.

1 tablespoon butter or margarine
12 ounces crabmeat, picked clean
¼ cup sherry
¼ cup milk
¼ cup whipping (heavy) cream
2 egg yolks
½ teaspoon cayenne pepper
Salt and pepper to taste
6 toasted English-style muffins
Lemon wedges (as garnish)

1 Heat the butter in a wide skillet over medium-high heat. Add the crabmeat and stir until heated through. Add the sherry and simmer another 3 minutes.

2 In a bowl, beat the milk, cream, egg yolks, cayenne, salt, and pepper. Add to the skillet. Reduce the heat to medium, and simmer, stirring occasionally, until the sauce thickens, about 3 to 5 minutes.

3 Spoon over toasted muffin halves and serve hot with lemon wedges.

Chinese Shrimp and Scallop Skewers

This one works just as well steamed in the dead of winter as it does on a summer grill. The sweet-and-sour sauce adds just the right tanginess, without overpowering the seafood. You might try the sauce with your favorite fish, as well.

Recipe is for each skewer; increase amounts needed for number of skewers desired

PER SKEWER

3 large sea scallops

2 chunks jumbo shrimp (you'll probably want to cut the shrimp in half)

2 to 4 1-inch square pieces of green and red bell pepper

2 or 3 small onions, outer layers peeled

2 tomato wedges

CHINESE SWEET AND SOUR SAUCE

½ cup pineapple juice

3 tablespoons oil

2 tablespoons brown sugar

1 teaspoon soy sauce

½ teaspoon black pepper

¼ cup mild vinegar

Hot cooked rice

1 Arrange the skewer ingredients on an 8- or 10-inch bamboo skewer for best presentation of shape and color. Use the peppers to separate the seafood.

2 Steam the skewer, or poach in a little white wine, or grill over hot coals.

3 In a saucepan over medium heat, combine ingredients for sauce. Stir until thickened, then use to baste skewer once.

4 Serve with rice, and the Chinese sweet-and-sour sauce for dipping or pouring over the skewers.

Shrimp Creole

Makes 4 to 6 servings

In the mid-to-late eighteenth century, the Spanish were desperately trying to populate the small colonies in Louisiana that had been given to them by Louis XV, after he had determined that they were too much trouble. The Acadian settlers imported from France became known as Cajuns, and went into the bayou country outside of New Orleans. Anyone of European descent who was left in New Orleans was called Criollos, a name that eventually became Creole.

Creole or Cajun, the cuisine relies on one thing: the roux. It's a mixture of oil and flour that must be browned perfectly to add that special "something" to the dishes prepared. Though most Creole cooks believe a roux should be brought to its nut-brown color slowly, if you're careful you can speed the process quite efficiently. The result is spectacular, and the flavor cannot be matched in any other cuisine.

This recipe is a compilation of many that I've come across, with recent input from Paul Prudhomme, and takes the least amount of time to prepare. Though you'll want to simmer this for a good half-hour or more, you'll have all the ingredients, save the shrimp, in the pot in minutes.

⅓ cup vegetable oil
⅓ cup all-purpose flour
6 green onions, chopped (reserve 1 to 2 tablespoons for garnish)
1 large onion, chopped
2 medium green bell peppers, chopped
4 garlic cloves, minced
3 celery stalks, chopped
6 large tomatoes, peeled and chopped
1½ cups Burgundy wine
1 8-ounce bottle clam juice

1 Prepare the roux in a heavy skillet by heating the oil over medium-high heat. Then add the flour all at once, and stir quickly to combine the oil and flour. Paul Prudhomme suggests we frequently scrape the bottom of the pan, continually turning the rich, browned bits of roux. Cook, stirring constantly, so the roux does not burn, until it is a nutty brown color, about 5 minutes.

2 Add the green onions, onion, green peppers, garlic, and celery. Sauté until the vegetables are thoroughly wilted, then stir in the tomatoes and wine. Cook, stirring often, until the liquid is reduced by half. Stir in the clam juice, bay leaf,

1 large bay leaf, crushed
¾ tablespoon dried thyme
1 tablespoon minced fresh parsley
½ teaspoon black pepper
½ teaspoon cayenne pepper
Salt to taste
3 pounds medium shrimp, peeled and deveined
Juice of 1 lemon
Hot cooked rice

thyme, parsley, black pepper, cayenne, and salt to taste. Cover and cook over medium-low heat for 30 minutes, stirring occasionally.

3 Stir in the shrimp and the lemon juice. When shrimp are coral pink, in about 3 minutes, the dish is ready. Serve over rice, sprinkled with some of the reserved green onions and the parsley.

Garlic-Ease

If time is truly of the essence, it makes good sense to keep a jar of minced garlic in the refrigerator. There are many good brands available in most markets, or you can make some of your own when you have a moment. It saves the time of peeling and mincing.

Shrimp with a Lobster Sauce

Makes 4 servings

The name of the sauce in this dish is a deceit. There is no lobster in it at all. It's actually a sauce created by the Cantonese chefs to accompany their lobster dishes, but was long ago adapted for other dishes as well. But lobster? Sorry. There are many fine versions of this dish, especially in oriental cookbooks. This version was adapted from *Betty Crocker's New International Cookbook.*

3 garlic cloves, finely chopped
2 tablespoons soy sauce
1 tablespoon black beans, mashed
1 teaspoon finely chopped fresh ginger
1 teaspoon sugar
½ teaspoon salt
2 tablespoons vegetable oil
1 pound shrimp, shelled and deveined
2 green onions, chopped (reserve tops for garnish)
½ cup hot water
1 tablespoon cornstarch
2 eggs, beaten
Hot cooked rice

1 In a bowl, combine the garlic, soy sauce, beans, ginger, sugar, and salt.

2 Heat the oil in a wok or large skillet over medium-high heat until very hot. Stir in the shrimp, bean mixture, and green onions. Cook for 1 minute. Stir in the hot water. Cover and cook until shrimp are coral pink, about 3 to 5 minutes.

3 Take 1 tablespoon of the cooking liquid and mix it with the cornstarch in a measuring cup. When blended, add to the pan. Add the eggs and cook until the eggs are set, 2 minutes.

4 Serve over hot rice, sprinkled with the reserved green onion tops.

A Quick Thicken

To quickly thicken a sauce, do not just add the thickening agent—be it flour or cornstarch—to the pan. It will more than likely form small balls that take forever to break up. Instead, remove 1 or 2 tablespoons of the heated liquid from the pot, and in a small bowl, combine it with the flour or cornstarch, which will quickly dissolve and blend. Then stir it back into the pan.

Quick Shrimp and Vegetables Mediterranean

Makes 4 servings

This is one of those great recipes that has nothing remarkable about it except the final result. Easy to prep, quick to prepare—but it has a wonderful mix of herbs for the palate and colors for the eye. I came across the dish on a Caribbean cruise ship several years ago, and was pleasantly surprised when the cook showed me how easy it was to prepare.

3 to 4 tablespoons butter or margarine
2 tablespoons olive oil
2 garlic cloves, chopped
2 green onions, finely minced (including tops)
½ medium carrot, in ⅛-inch round slices
8 to 10 green beans, cut into 1-inch lengths
½ red bell pepper, cut into ½-inch squares
½ Bermuda onion, sliced, then quartered
Dry white wine
1 pound large shrimp, peeled, deveined, and cut into bite-size pieces
½ teaspoon chopped dried thyme
½ teaspoon chopped dried basil
1 teaspoon chopped dried chives
½ teaspoon chopped dried oregano
Hot cooked rice
Lemon wedges

1 In a large saucepan, melt together the butter or margarine and 1 tablespoon of the olive oil over medium-high heat. Drop in 1 garlic clove and the green onions and cook until the onions wilt, about 1 to 2 minutes.

2 Add the carrot and cook for about 2 or 3 minutes. Then successively add the green beans, red pepper, and Bermuda onion, cooking for 1 minute or so after adding each vegetable. You want the vegetables crisp, colorful, and hot. Add 2 tablespoons dry white wine or water if the vegetables seem a bit dry—the liquid will steam and aid in the flavor and vividness of the colors.

3 About the time you begin adding the vegetables to the butter, oil, and garlic mixture, put the other 1 tablespoon of olive oil and the other garlic clove in a large skillet over medium-high heat. Add the shrimp and sauté, turning the pieces frequently, until they are a bright coral color, about 2 to 3 minutes.

4 Add the shrimp and herbs to the saucepan with the vegetables and mix well, cooking for another 2 or 3 minutes. Serve over a bed of hot rice. Squeeze a small wedge of lemon over each plate immediately before serving.

Prawns Early Morning

Prawns Early Morning, created by Patrice Boely of New York's Polo Restaurant, takes its name from the color of the dish's sauce—that beautiful mix of red, orange, and coral that singes the horizon just as the sun is coming up. I have slightly modified the presentation of the shrimp in the sauce, but have not touched the perfect mix of ingredients.

1½ pounds extra-large shrimp, peeled and deveined
2 tablespoons butter or margarine
1 tablespoon chopped shallot
¼ cup dry white wine
Salt and pepper to taste
1 tablespoon chopped fresh parsley
1 teaspoon tomato paste
⅓ cup heavy cream
⅛ teaspoon chopped dried thyme
Several thyme sprigs

1 Peel and devein the shrimp, then pat dry. Heat the butter or margarine in a large skillet over medium to high heat until brown. Add the shrimp and sauté for 2 minutes on each side. Remove the shrimp from the skillet and keep warm.

2 Add the chopped shallot to the skillet and sauté for 1 minute.

3 Combine the wine, salt, pepper, parsley, and tomato paste in a bowl, then add to the skillet and cook over medium heat for about 5 minutes or until reduced to about 1 tablespoon. Add the cream and chopped thyme and boil for 3 minutes. Remove the skillet from the heat and strain the sauce to catch as much of the parsley and thyme as possible.

4 Spread a thin layer of the sauce on each serving plate, so it just covers the center area out to the border. Arrange 4 or 5 shrimp in a circle on the plate, setting them gently onto the sauce so as not to disturb it. Sprinkle 2 or 3 one-inch sections of thyme sprigs over the plate and serve.

Lose the Shells

Always remove the shells from your shellfish and mollusks when you can do so. It will speed the cooking of the shrimp, lobster, clams, or oysters. Unless the recipe specifically calls for the shells on, adapt a bit and remove them.

Scallop and Vegetable Pesto Sauté

Makes 2 servings

3 tablespoons butter or margarine
1 medium carrot, cut into ¼-inch slices
1 small onion, coarsely chopped
1 small zucchini, in ¼-inch slices
8 to 10 small fresh mushrooms, halved
1 small green bell pepper, seeded and coarsely chopped
2 to 3 tablespoons fresh Pesto (recipe follows)
¾ pound sea scallops, rinsed, patted dry, and cut into ¼-inch-thick slices
Salt to taste
Grated Parmesan cheese

Pesto is said to have been created in Genoa, Italy, though a similar sauce known as *pistou* hails from France, along the Riviera. It's a rich mixture of basil, garlic, pine nuts, oil, and cheese, and is one of the most distinctive tastes in Italian cooking. Though there are many fine commercial versions of pesto, making it fresh is really the only way to have it electrify a dish like this.

1 Melt 2 tablespoons of the butter or margarine in a wide frying pan over medium-high heat. Add the carrot and onion, and cook for 2 to 3 minutes. Add the zucchini, mushrooms, and pepper and continue to cook. Stir frequently. When vegetables are just crisp-tender, in 3 to 4 minutes, remove from the pan and keep warm.

2 Melt remaining 1 tablespoon of butter or margarine in the pan, and stir in the pesto. Add the scallops immediately and cook them until they are just cooked through, about 4 minutes. Return the vegetables to the pan and cook until dish is heated through. Season with salt.

3 Sprinkle with the Parmesan cheese before serving.

Pesto Sauce

PESTO SAUCE
⅔ cup coarsely chopped and packed basil leaves
⅓ cup grated Parmesan cheese
⅓ cup olive oil
2 tablespoons pine nuts
½ teaspoon salt
⅛ teaspoon pepper
1 garlic clove

Prepare the pesto sauce by placing all its ingredients in a blender. Cover and blend on high speed until sauce is smooth and thoroughly mixed.

Jarred Sauces

If time is of the essence, consider using jarred sauces like pesto. There are many good ones easily found in the market, and most of them will deliver the fresh flavors you desire.

Quick and Exceptional Sauces for Fish

Nothing enhances a seafood dish like an exceptional sauce. It can help mask the natural flavor of the flesh for those who are not big fans, and can add a refreshing or distinctive surprise for those who can't get enough of the fruits of the sea.

Each of the following sauces and marinades takes very little time to prepare; most can be created in just a few minutes. Where the sauce is best with a specific fish, I have identified it. Otherwise, experiment with them—see how easy it is to surprise yourself and your guests, simply by adding a quick and exceptional sauce.

Orange-Shallot Sauce

Makes about 2½ cups

Good for haddock, cod, scrod, or flounder.

1 ¼ pounds butter or margarine
1 large shallot, minced extremely fine
Juice of 3 large oranges (every drop you can get)
Zest from the orange peels

1 Melt ½ cup of butter or margarine in a large non-aluminum saucepan over medium heat. Add the shallot and sauté for 3 minutes.

2 Add the juice from the oranges, and bring to a boil. Reduce the heat and add the orange zest.

3 Slowly whisk in the remaining butter or margarine 1 tablespoon at a time. Stir constantly until sauce has thickened. Pour over fish to serve.

Tapenade

Makes about 1 cup

Tapenade is a garlic and olive paste traditionally found in the south of France. It's a marvelous way to add some life to any typical white-fleshed fish.

1 8-ounce can pitted ripe olives, drained
2 or 3 garlic cloves
6 tablespoons olive oil

1 Combine the olives and the garlic in a food processor or blender. Whirl on high until finely minced.

2 Add the olive oil in a steady stream while processor is in motion. Don't overdo the oil. Stop when the mixture forms a paste, even if all the oil is not used.

3 Spoon the tapenade over the fish. It can be added in the last minute of broiling or poaching, or added at the table.

Dijon Dill Dipping and Grilling Sauce

Makes slightly under 3 cups

One of my favorite sauces. The Dijon mustard is snappy and dominant, but the dill adds just the right balance—it doesn't let the Dijon overpower the fish or seafood. Great for kebobs that include shrimp or scallops.

¼ cup Dijon mustard
2 tablespoons white wine vinegar
1 tablespoon sugar
½ cup chopped fresh dill, or 1 tablespoon dried
1 cup olive or vege-table oil

1 In a small bowl, mix the mustard, vinegar, sugar, and dill. Slowly add the oil, about a tablespoon at a time, stirring the dressing constantly.

2 The sauce is best if refrigerated for at least 2 hours to let the flavors work together, but you can use it immediately, if needed.

Garlic-Dijon Sauce

Makes about 1 ¼ cups

This is a great sauce best used with poached fish. Patrice Boely suggests it for any white-fleshed fish, but I think you can include tuna or snapper as well. It's similar to the Dijon dipping sauce, but the twelve cloves of garlic set it apart quite distinctively.

12 garlic cloves, peeled
  and pureed
2 large egg yolks
1 teaspoon Dijon
  mustard
1 cup virgin olive oil
Salt and freshly ground
  pepper to taste

1 In a mixing bowl, combine the garlic and egg yolks with the mustard. Slowly add the oil, whisking or stirring constantly. Continue to stir until the sauce achieves a mayonnaiselike consistency.

2 Season with salt and pepper and stir one final time before spooning onto fish.

Fast Tomato Sauce

Makes about 2 cups

Another wonderful sauce from Patrice Boely. I've used this one more times than I can remember, adapting it a little here, a little there. It's quite nice for pasta, too, or with green beans.

2 tablespoons olive oil
1 small white onion,
  chopped
1 celery stalk, chopped
1 small carrot, peeled
  and thinly sliced
2 garlic cloves, minced
¼ teaspoon dried thyme
1 bay leaf
5 ripe tomatoes, sliced
1 teaspoon chicken broth
¼ chicken bouillon cube
Salt and freshly ground
  pepper

1 Heat the olive oil in a saucepan over high heat. Add the onion, celery, carrot, garlic, thyme, and bay leaf. Sauté for 3 to 5 minutes. Add the remaining ingredients and cook for another 5 to 8 minutes.

2 Discard the bay leaf, and put the sauce in a food processor or blender and puree.

3 Reheat the sauce in a saucepan before using.

Shrimp Sauce

Makes about 3 cups

What a sauce this is! It's particularly good for baked fish, or for pouring over a fillet and flash broiling it. It is extremely simple to make, and will get you raves when you serve it.

2 cups tomato sauce
1 teaspoon Worcestershire sauce
1 teaspoon dried tarragon
¼ cup chopped pitted olives
½ cup chopped cooked shrimp
½ cup sautéed mushrooms
¼ cup finely chopped celery

Heat the tomato sauce to boiling. Add all other ingredients, then reduce heat and simmer for 10 to 15 minutes. Spoon over fish as described above.

Rockport Red Sauce

Makes about 1 cup

This is a terrific fish sauce that came to me from Ms. E. Howell, a viewer in Houston, Texas. She says it's one of the better sauces found down her way, and I have to agree.

1 cup chili sauce
3 tablespoons lemon juice
1 tablespoon horseradish
3 drops Tabasco or other hot pepper sauce
½ teaspoon celery salt
⅛ teaspoon salt

Combine all ingredients and use immediately for fillets, or chill as a cocktail sauce for shrimp or crab.

Chicken, Turkey, Beef, Pork, and Lamb

The discovery of a new dish does more for human happiness than the discovery of a new star.

—Anthelme Brillat-Savarin

Regardless of what precedes or follows it, the main dish we serve is going to be the focus of the meal. And as Brillat-Savarin implies, new dishes—at least new to us—are always going to be welcome. In this section I've assembled a number of dishes I found particularly intriguing. Some were new to me, and adapted to my requirements on *In the Kitchen with Bob.* Others I've enjoyed for a number of years, but are more than likely new to you, as they are personal family dishes.

The wonder of chicken is in what you can do with it. Or perhaps it's better to say there's not really too much you *can't* do with it. It's adaptable to virtually any situation. For the most part, I use boneless, skinless breasts for the recipes, as they cook much more quickly, but you shouldn't let that prevent you from trying some of the ideas with bone-in chicken parts. For instance, the spicy-hot Chicken Escabeche or the tangy Chicken Breasts in Orange Sauce can be prepared either way. The Poulet Paysan may be the simplest and most traditional of the preparations included, requiring just a stockpot, ten minutes of prep time, and a little simmering. For the extraordinary, enjoy the Chicken in Walnut Sauce, a Russian dish swimming in a rich mix of walnuts, spices, and pomegranate juice, or the simple Singapore Chicken, with its superb balance and oriental sensibility.

The turkey dishes included here are the most requested from my annual Thanksgiving Day programs, "What Are You Gonna Do with All That Turkey?" They are all adaptations that use leftover turkey in new and exciting ways (though you can use fresh turkey if you'd prefer). From the creamy, cheesy silkiness of the Turkey Elegant to the fruity Turkey Breast with Raspberry Glaze, you'll find several preferable alternatives to just reheating the Thanksgiving bird.

Finally, though I don't eat much beef, pork, or lamb, there are a few dishes I will go out of my way for. One is Rinderrouladen, a classic German dish of stuffed beef rolls that I was introduced to on a recent trip to Germany; another is the hot and peppery Beef in Pepper Sauce, an Ethiopian dish that blends perfectly red pepper, jalapeños, bell peppers, and spices. The Pork and Green Onion Stir-Fry is one of the few dishes I've found that makes excellent use of the light, sharp zing of the green onion, and the Lamb Curry wonderfully mixes succulent lamb, tart green apples, and spicy curry.

Poulet Paysan

French for "peasant chicken," Poulet Paysan is one of the simplest ways to prepare a chicken dinner. French peasants toss a chicken in the pot along with whatever vegetables they happen to have in the garden or find fresh in the market that day. A little water, a little heat, a little time . . . and *voilà!*

There really isn't any "right" way to make Poulet Paysan. As do the French peasants, use what you have. This version is cooked in the Bowersox household at least once a week. We usually have enough meat, vegetables, and stock to make a light soup for the next day's lunch. There's hardly any effort, either—once it's in the pot, your work is *fini.*

1 3- to 5-pound chicken
6 to 8 medium potatoes, quartered
4 or 5 medium onions, quartered
6 to 8 medium carrots, cut into 2-inch lengths
4 to 6 celery stalks, cut into 2-inch lengths
1 cup dry white wine
2 teaspoons dried tarragon
1 teaspoon dried basil
Salt and pepper to taste
1 chicken bouillon cube (optional, for heavier flavor)
1 teaball of black peppercorns

1 Wash and clean the chicken thoroughly. I suggest you remove all skin and fat except the skin on the wings of the chicken. You need a little for flavor. Put the chicken in a stockpot or Dutch oven large enough to hold it with room around it.

2 Place the potatoes, onions, carrots, and celery around the chicken. Add enough water to just cover the vegetables. Add the wine, tarragon, basil, salt, and pepper. If you wish to use the bouillon, add it now as well. Hang the teaball of peppercorns from the side of the pot, making sure that it is well under the water.

3 Bring to a boil over high heat, then reduce heat to achieve a simmer. Simmer for 90 minutes, or until chicken is cooked through.

4 Center the chicken on a platter and surround with the vegetables. Serve hot. If you wish, you can make a gravy with some of the stock created by the cooking.

Chicken Diane

Makes 4 servings

4 large boneless chicken breasts
Salt and pepper to taste
2 tablespoons light vegetable oil
3 tablespoons chopped green onions, including white and light-green tops
Juice of ½ lime
2 tablespoons brandy
3 tablespoons chopped fresh parsley
2 teaspoons Dijon mustard
¼ cup chicken broth
2 tablespoons butter or margarine

This is one of the classics for chicken. It's a haute cuisine recipe that prepares in minutes. The green onions and the brandy make this version a tangy, rich one. It's fabulous with broccoli as a side dish.

1 Place each chicken breast between 2 sheets of waxed paper. With a wooden mallet, pound the breasts lightly to a thickness of approximately ¼ inch. Make sure not to break them apart. Sprinkle with salt and pepper.

2 Put 1 tablespoon of oil and 1 tablespoon of the butter or margarine in a large skillet over medium-high heat. Add the chicken and sauté for 2 to 3 minutes on a side. Remove and keep warm.

3 To the juices in the skillet, add the green onions, lime juice, brandy, parsley, and mustard. Cook for 15 seconds, whisking constantly. Stir in the broth, stirring until smooth, then add the butter or margarine and remaining oil.

4 Add the chicken again long enough to warm it, then serve. Place the chicken on serving plates, and spoon the sauce over them.

Pound Them

One of the easiest ways to speed a boneless chicken breast recipe along is to alter the thickness of the chicken breasts. Place the breasts between 2 pieces of waxed paper and, using a wooden mallet (or large serving spoon if you don't have a mallet), pound the breast meat to a thickness of under ¼ inch. Try not to tear the meat while doing this. You'll find the chicken will cook almost twice as fast.

Two Polish Chicken Dishes

My grandmother-in-law, Martha Marshall, is a spry eighty-year-old Polish lady who's forgotten more terrific recipes than this cookbook holds. She's one of those enviable cooks who never reaches for a measuring cup or spoon. She does it all with her hands: teaspoons of this, tablespoons of that—it's always right on the money, though when asked she'll tell you she doesn't know amounts. "I just put it in," she says.

Two of my favorite "Granny" recipes follow. The first, Chicken Paprika, is a traditional Polish rendering of chicken. It's quick and easy to prepare, and has a bite to it that you'll learn to love. The second she gave me one summer afternoon when I was in search of something different to put on the barbecue. I've dubbed it Chicken Lendzioszek, after Granny's married name.

Chicken Paprika

1 tablespoon butter or margarine
3 or 4 boneless, skinless chicken breasts, cut into strips 1 inch wide
1 medium onion, sliced
1 teaspoon ground paprika
Salt and pepper to taste
¾ cup chicken broth
2 tablespoons sour cream
1 teaspoon flour

1 Melt the butter or margarine in a skillet over medium-high heat and add the chicken. Sauté for 3 to 5 minutes, then remove and set aside on a warm platter or dish.

2 In the skillet with the chicken juices, add the onion, paprika, and salt and pepper. Sauté until the onion is translucent, about 1 to 2 minutes. Return the chicken to the skillet, and add the broth. Cover and simmer for 5 to 8 minutes. Remove the chicken again, setting it out on the serving platter.

3 Mix the sour cream with the flour, then add to the skillet juices. Cook over high heat for 2 to 3 minutes or until sauce thickens. Pour over the chicken and serve.

Chicken Lendzioszek

1 18-ounce bottle
barbecue sauce (we
use Kraft Original)
1 8-ounce jar Dijon
mustard
½ 17-ounce container
honey
3 pounds boneless
chicken tenders
(or boneless breast,
cut into strips)

1 In a large mixing bowl, combine the barbecue sauce, mustard, and honey. Mix it thoroughly.

2 Place the tenders or strips in the sauce, and turn until all pieces of chicken are coated. Place the chicken on a hot barbecue or in a large skillet over high heat. The chicken tenders will cook almost immediately. The longer you leave them on the grill or in the pan, the darker the flavor of the sauce. Serve immediately as a finger food or as the meat of the entree.

Chicken in Walnut Sauce

Makes 6 servings

I found this Russian treat in *Betty Crocker's New International Cookbook,* and fell in love with it the first time I prepared it on the air. It uses pomegranate juice, walnuts, and an unusual mix of herbs to achieve its individual flavor. Serve it with rice and a green vegetable for a colorful plate.

**2 tablespoons vege-
table oil**
**2½ pounds boneless,
skinless chicken breasts**
1 large onion, chopped
**¾ cup finely chopped
walnuts**
**¾ cup unsweetened
pomegranate juice**
¼ cup water
**1 teaspoon ground
cinnamon**
½ teaspoon salt
**¼ teaspoon ground
coriander**
**⅛ teaspoon ground
allspice**
⅛ teaspoon pepper

1 Heat the oil in a large skillet or frying pan. Cook the chicken over medium-high heat until it is brown on both sides, about 3 to 4 minutes. Remove to a warm dish.

2 To the juices in the skillet add the onion and cook until wilted, about 1 to 2 minutes. Stir in the remaining ingredients and cook for 1 to 2 minutes.

3 Return the chicken to the skillet. Heat to boiling, then reduce heat to medium. Simmer until chicken is done, about 4 or 5 minutes.

4 Remove the chicken to a warm serving platter with a slotted spoon, leaving all liquid in the skillet. Heat the juices to boiling, stirring occasionally, until slightly reduced and thickened. Spoon the sauce over the chicken.

Pineapple Chicken

Makes 6 servings

This dish is one that I found to satisfy my memory of another chicken dish I had on one of my many trips to the Caribbean. I think what I remembered most was the freshness and sweetness of the pineapple; it washed every bite. This version, however, includes some extra touches that make it special: the sherry, cinnamon, and cloves are nuances the original Caribbean dish lacked.

2 tablespoons olive oil
1 medium onion, chopped
3 pounds boneless, skinless chicken breasts, chunked or stripped
1 16-ounce can pineapple chunks, drained
½ cup dry sherry
2 tablespoons cider or red wine vinegar
1 teaspoon salt
¼ teaspoon ground cinnamon
¼ teaspoon ground cloves
⅛ teaspoon pepper
2 medium tomatoes, chopped

1 In a large skillet or frying pan, heat the oil over medium-high heat until hot. Add the onion and garlic and cook until the onion wilts, about 1 to 2 minutes. Add the chicken, and cook for about 5 minutes, turning chicken so it browns evenly.

2 Add the pineapple, sherry, vinegar, salt, cinnamon, cloves, and pepper. Stir to blend and to coat chicken pieces. Simmer vigorously for 3 to 4 minutes. Don't overdo the heat; you don't want the pineapple chunks to break down.

3 Add the tomatoes and simmer another 2 minutes, or until they are warm. Serve hot.

Hot, Hot, Hot

I always make sure my pan is hot before I begin my cooking. I warm it to a fairly high temperature, so that I hit the ground running. Along those same lines, I usually cook over high heat, which greatly speeds my cooking. Of course, this requires a bit more concentration and careful control, but the reward is a faster meal.

Chicken with Peaches

Makes 4 servings

2 tablespoons oil
2½ pounds boneless,
  skinless chicken, a mix
  of breast and thigh
  meats, cut into
  finger-sized strips
1 teaspoon salt
½ teaspoon five-spice
  powder
1 garlic clove, minced
  very fine
1 8-ounce can sliced
  peaches, liquid
  included
1 tablespoon sugar
2 tablespoons lemon
  juice
½ cup chicken broth
2 teaspoons cornstarch
1 tablespoon water
12 ounces snowpeas
Hot cooked rice

This is one of the most elegant yet simplest dishes to make. The colors of the peaches and the snowpeas are perfect together, making it a beautiful dish as well. It was specially designed to cook quickly in a wok or wok frying pan, and would be equally as delicious made with turkey.

1 Heat a wok or wok frying pan over medium-high to high heat. Add 1 tablespoon of oil. When the oil is hot, add the chicken, salt, and five-spice powder, and stir-fry for 4 to 5 minutes. Turn often, browning on all sides. Remove from wok and keep warm.

2 Add remaining 1 tablespoon oil to wok and heat. Add the garlic and stir-fry until just brown. Add the peaches and sugar, stirring until the sugar is melted and peaches are warm, then add the lemon juice and broth. Bring to a boil.

3 Mix the cornstarch with the water, blend thoroughly, then add to the wok and stir in immediately. Add the snowpeas, cover, and steam for 30 seconds. Return the chicken to the wok and stir in. Cover and steam until chicken is reheated, 1 to 2 minutes. Serve over hot rice.

Chicken Escabeche

Makes 4 servings

ESCABECHE PASTE
- 8 garlic cloves, minced
- 1 teaspoon ground allspice
- 1 teaspoon ground cloves
- 1 teaspoon ground cumin
- 1 teaspoon ground coriander
- 1½ teaspoons ground cinnamon
- ¾ teaspoon coarsely ground black pepper
- 2 teaspoons dried oregano
- ¼ teaspoon cayenne pepper
- 2 tablespoons orange juice
- 2 tablespoons white wine vinegar

- 3 pounds boneless, skinless chicken breast
- 2 tablespoons light olive oil
- 2 large onions, thinly sliced
- ¾ cup diced green chili peppers
- 1¼ cups chicken broth
- 1½ tablespoons cornstarch
- 1½ tablespoons warm water
- 3 tablespoons fresh chopped cilantro or 1 tablespoon dried

Escabeche is a remarkable mix of garlic and spices—an instant hit with cooks like me who experiment with spice combinations. That it has a little bite to it doesn't hurt, either.

I first learned about escabeche sauce (or paste) in Penelope Casas's extraordinary book on Spanish *tapas* cooking. The sauce was used by the Spanish nearly half a century ago as a presevative in an age of no refrigeration. They used it with fowl and fish. Today we don't have to worry about preservation; we get to enjoy the escabeche for the spicy flavor it adds.

1 Prepare the escabeche paste by combining all ingredients in small bowl. Stir to mix thoroughly.

2 Trim the chicken breasts of all fat, rinse them, and pat dry. Rub the escabeche paste over both sides of each breast. Piercing the breast several times with a fork or knife point will help infuse the paste's flavors deep into the meat.

3 In a large frying pan, heat 1 tablespoon of the oil over medium-high heat and add the breasts. Turn to set the paste on both sides.

4 Meanwhile, in a saucepan, heat the remaining 1 tablespoon of the oil over medium heat. Add the onions and cook until they wilt, about 1 to 2 minutes. Add the chilies and broth, and cook, stirring occasionally. Mix the cornstarch with the water, blending thoroughly, then add to the saucepan. Cook and stir until sauce thickens. Stir in the cilantro and cook for 1 minute more.

5 Serve chicken hot. Spoon sauce over individual portions.

Singapore Chicken

Singapore Chicken is a light, quick meal for two, with a distinctive nuttiness often found in oriental cooking. Another nice mix of spices—including the rarely used lemongrass—endeared this recipe to me, though I've long forgotten how I came by the dish. Suffice it to say that I'm happy it's in my files.

4 small red onions, chopped
2 garlic cloves, minced
4 teaspoons minced lemongrass
1 teaspoon ground coriander
1 teaspoon ground cumin
1 teaspoon ground ginger
Salt to taste
Sugar to taste
1 pound boneless chicken breasts, in finger-size strips
1 tablespoon light vegetable oil

1 In a food processor or blender, combine the onions, garlic, lemongrass, coriander, cumin, and ginger. Blend until smooth. Pour into a large bowl and stir in salt and sugar to taste. Add the chicken and marinate, refrigerated, for about 1 hour.

2 In a large skillet, heat the vegetable oil over medium-high heat. Add the chicken and stir-fry until cooked through, about 4 to 5 minutes.

NUT SAUCE
2 small red onions, chopped
4 small dried red chili peppers
1 garlic clove
2 macadamia nuts
⅛ cup peanut oil
¾ cup ground peanuts
2 tablespoons lemon juice
6 tablespoons water
Salt to taste
Sugar to taste

3 Meanwhile, make the nut sauce. In a food processor or blender, combine the onions, chilies, garlic, and nuts. Mix until a smooth paste is formed.

4 Heat the peanut oil in a saucepan over medium-high heat. Add the nut puree and cook until warm. Stir in the ground peanuts and the lemon juice. Add the water and salt and sugar to taste. Bring to a boil and thicken slightly.

5 Arrange the chicken strips on a serving platter, and pour the sauce over them. Serve hot.

Chicken Breasts in Orange Sauce

Makes 3 servings

It really doesn't get too much easier than this. A couple of minutes in preparation, and the oven does the rest.

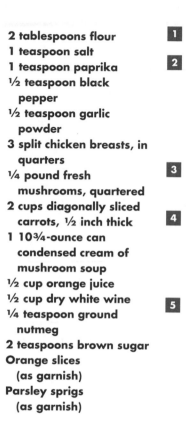

2 tablespoons flour
1 teaspoon salt
1 teaspoon paprika
½ teaspoon black
  pepper
½ teaspoon garlic
  powder
3 split chicken breasts, in
  quarters
¼ pound fresh
  mushrooms, quartered
2 cups diagonally sliced
  carrots, ½ inch thick
1 10¾-ounce can
  condensed cream of
  mushroom soup
½ cup orange juice
½ cup dry white wine
¼ teaspoon ground
  nutmeg
2 teaspoons brown sugar
Orange slices
  (as garnish)
Parsley sprigs
  (as garnish)

1 Preheat the oven to 350 degrees.

2 In a small bag, combine the flour, salt, paprika, pepper, and garlic powder. After rinsing the chicken breasts and shaking off any excess water, place them in the bag and coat completely with the spice mixture. Place the breasts in a 3-quart casserole.

3 Scatter the mushrooms and carrots around and on top of the breasts.

4 In a bowl, combine the soup, orange juice, wine, nutmeg, and brown sugar. Stir into a smooth syrup. Spoon the mixture over the chicken and vegetables. Your work is now finished.

5 Bake, covered, for 30 to 40 minutes. Serve with orange slices and parsley sprigs.

Plan Your Leftovers

It pays to plan your leftovers deliberately. Buy more of your main ingredients than you need, so you'll have some for a "planned leftover" meal that cooks quickly. Or plan it so that the leftovers from two different meals can be quickly and easily combined into a third meal.

Chicken and Vegetable Stir-Fry

Makes 6 servings

1 tablespoon vege-
table oil
2 garlic cloves, chopped
2 pounds boneless
chicken breast, cut into
bite-size chunks
⅓ cup dry white wine
1 cup sliced carrots, 1
inch long and ¼ inch
thick
1 cup broccoli flowerettes
1 cup cauliflower
flowerettes
½ cup *each* sliced green,
red, and yellow bell
pepper, cut 1 inch long
and ¼ inch wide
1 cup sliced celery, cut 1
inch long and
¼ inch wide
10 to 12 snowpeas
6 large mushrooms,
quartered
½ Bermuda onion, sliced
into ¼-inch-wide rings
¼ cup sugar
1 teaspoon dried basil
1 teaspoon dried
tarragon
½ cup soy sauce
Juice of 1 lemon
Hot cooked rice

A quick, one-pan dish, this is my Americanization of an oriental classic. Most stir-fries found in traditional Chinese or Japanese restaurants are cooked with a great deal of pork fat, and are often cooked in large batches, sitting in the kitchen for several hours until ordered. The vegetables often are wilted and mushy. I wanted my vegetables to be crisp and the fat content to be low. Most of the cooking time is in the prep—cutting the vegetables. I suggest you do all the prep first, then cook. You'll be sitting and eating in ten minutes.

1 In a large 4-quart skillet, wok, or stockpot, heat the oil over medium-high heat. Add the garlic and cook until brown. Immediately add the chicken and stir-fry, turning constantly, until nearly cooked through, about 5 minutes.

2 Add the wine and bring to a vigorous simmer. You will now actually be steaming the vegetables from this point on. After adding each vegetable, cover and steam for 1 to 2 minutes, then continue. If you need extra liquid, you can add a bit more wine or a little water. Be conservative, though, as the vegetables will begin adding their own liquid to the pan, and you don't want to drown the dish. First add the carrots, cover, and steam for 1 to 2 minutes. Then, in succession, add the broccoli and cauliflower together, stir, cover, and steam; then the peppers, stir, cover, and steam; the snowpeas, stir, cover, and steam; the celery, stir, cover, and steam, then the mushrooms and onion, stir, cover, and steam.

3 Add the sugar, basil, tarragon, and soy sauce; stir. Just before serving, squeeze the juice of 1 lemon over the dish and toss one last time to mix thoroughly. Serve over hot rice with soy sauce on the table.

Chicken Sauté Bourguignonne

Makes 4 to 6 servings

The Burgundy region of France is one of the great wine-producing areas of the world. The Burgundies produced there are rich and dark with flavor, and this hasn't been lost on chefs down through the years. Bourguignonne dishes are essentially cooked in a Burgundy wine, and adding a subtle touch with a spice or two can yield a spectacular combination.

Such a dish is Craig Claiborne's Chicken Sauté Bourguignonne. I've adapted the recipe slightly to allow for speedier preparation, but the end results will be the same.

3 pounds boneless chicken breasts
4 tablespoons butter or margarine
½ pound fresh mushrooms, sliced
Salt and freshly ground pepper
½ cup finely chopped onion
1 tablespoon finely chopped shallot
1 bay leaf
1 garlic clove, minced
½ teaspoon dried thyme
1 tablespoon flour
½ cup chicken broth
1 cup Burgundy wine

1 Place the chicken breasts between 2 sheets of waxed paper and pound with a mallet until approximately ⅛ to ¼ inch thick. Try not to break the meat apart. Sprinkle the chicken with salt and pepper.

2 Heat 2 tablespoons of the butter in a heavy skillet over medium-high heat, and add the chicken. Cook for 5 minutes, turning to cook both sides. Transfer chicken to a warm dish.

3 To the juices remaining in the skillet add the mushrooms, salt, and pepper. Cook until the mushrooms take on color, about 2 minutes, then add the onion, shallot, bay leaf, garlic, and thyme. Cook, stirring for 1 minute. Sprinkle in the flour, stir to blend, then add the broth and the wine, stirring rapidly to blend. When smooth, add in the remaining butter and swirl to thicken the sauce slightly. Add the chicken and reheat the dish. Remove bay leaf.

4 Serve the chicken with the sauce spooned over it.

Turkey Elegant

Makes 3 servings

3 tablespoons butter or
  margarine
¼ cup chopped onion
3 tablespoons flour
2 cups half-and-half
½ teaspoon salt
½ teaspoon dried
  tarragon
1 cup grated Tillamook
  or Monterey Jack
  cheese
2 cups cubed cooked
  turkey (a mix of light
  and dark meats)
3 ounces fresh
  mushrooms, sliced
1 avocado, diced
Several large spinach
  leaves
6 avocado slices
Paprika

This dish is aptly named, for I believe turkey, well prepared, is one of the most elegant dishes we can serve. The addition of tarragon, cheese, and avocado further enhance the elegance here without forcing the dish to be heavy. It's a terrific way to make use of some of that leftover Thanksgiving turkey.

1 Melt the butter in a heavy skillet over medium heat. Add the onion and cook until soft, then add the flour and stir into the mix. Add the half-and-half, salt, and tarragon and continue cooking until the mixture thickens, about 2 to 3 minutes.

2 Add the cheese and cook, stirring constantly, until it is thoroughly melted. Stir in the turkey and mushrooms, and cook until heated through.

3 Peel, pit, and dice the avocado. Remove the skillet from the heat and carefully stir in the diced avocado, being careful not to break up the fruit.

4 Place spinach leaves on the individual serving plates. Spoon the Turkey Elegant into the center of the leaves. Place 2 slices of avocado on top of the turkey and sprinkle with the paprika.

Turkey Italiana

Makes 6 servings

4 tablespoons butter or margarine

10 fresh mushrooms, thinly sliced

¾ cup dry white wine

½ cup chicken stock

3 tablespoons chopped fresh parsley

Freshly ground white pepper to taste

2 tablespoons flour

6 slices turkey breast, ¼ to ⅜ inch thick (if uncooked, pound to thickness)

6 thin slices prosciutto

6 thin slices Fontina cheese

This has become a regular after-Thanksgiving dish for me. In a half-Italian household, the touches of prosciutto and Fontina cheese are a natural. It's quick and appreciated, and goes well with a little pasta and sautéed peppers.

1 In a saucepan over medium heat, place 2 tablespoons of the butter or margarine and the mushrooms. Sauté for about 3 minutes. Add the wine and cook until reduced by about one-fourth. Increase the heat to medium-high and add the stock, parsley, and pepper. Cook until reduced to about 1 cup. Reduce heat to low and keep warm until turkey is done.

2 Meanwhile, lightly flour the turkey, and shake off any excess. Melt the remaining 2 tablespoons of the butter or margarine in a large skillet over low heat. Add the turkey and sauté until lightly browned, about 4 to 5 minutes (or less if the turkey is precooked).

3 Top each slice of turkey with a slice of prosciutto and a slice of Fontina. Cover just until the cheese melts. Transfer to individual serving plates, and top each with some of the mushroom sauce.

Spiced Turkey Loaf

This is a nice way to use all those small pieces of turkey meat that you end up picking off the bones, or that fall to the side in the carving of the bird on its first night. The loaf is actually best if a mix of light and dark meats is used—the light meat helps keep the loaf a little drier, the dark imparts most of the flavor. The green olive gravy is a nice topper, too. Though the loaf must bake for about fifty minutes, you'll have it in the oven in just a few minutes.

GREEN OLIVE GRAVY
1 cup turkey gravy
½ cup chopped pitted green olives

1 ½ tablespoons grated onion
1 tablespoon butter or margarine
2 cups diced cooked turkey, a mix of light and dark meats
¾ teaspoon salt
1 cup cracker crumbs
¾ cup milk
2 eggs, beaten
½ cup finely chopped celery
¾ teaspoon chili powder
1 teaspoon thyme

1 Preheat the oven to 350 degrees. To make the green olive gravy, combine both ingredients in a saucepan and heat.

2 In a small frying pan, quickly sauté the grated onion in the butter or margarine until wilted, about 2 minutes. Use a medium heat, so it doesn't get overdone. You want it moist.

3 In a large bowl, place the sautéed onion, turkey, salt, cracker crumbs, milk, eggs, celery, chili powder, and thyme. Stir in the gravy. Mix the ingredients loosely—don't pack—and form into a loaf in a well-greased loaf pan.

4 Set the loaf pan in a second, larger pan of hot water, then place both in the oven. Bake for about 50 minutes.

5 Serve the loaf in slices, topped with the green olive gravy.

Turkey Breast
with Raspberry Glaze

Makes 2 to 4 servings

½ cup seedless
   raspberry jam
½ cup plus 1 tablespoon
   raspberry vinegar
5 tablespoons raspberry
   liqueur
¼ cup Dijon mustard
1 teaspoon grated
   orange peel
½ teaspoon dried thyme
4 cooked turkey breast
   slices, ¾ inch thick,
   trimmed to medallion
   size (or 4 fresh turkey
   breast tenderloins,
   about ¾ to 1 inch
   thick), about
   2 pounds total

This one's a snap, whether you're using cooked leftover turkey breast or uncooked breast tenderloins. All you really have to make is the glaze, which takes only minutes. I've seen many variations on this theme—I've tried to combine and simplify with this one.

1 In a 3-quart saucepan, combine the jam, 5 tablespoons vinegar, 1 tablespoon raspberry liqueur, mustard, orange peel, and thyme. Whisk well to blend, and bring to a boil over high heat. Cook, stirring, for 3 to 4 minutes, or until reduced by one-fourth. Keep warm.

2 Take ½ cup of the glaze from the saucepan and place in a medium bowl. Put the turkey (cooked or uncooked) in the bowl, and turn several times until well coated.

3 Combine the remaining ¼ cup raspberry vinegar and the remaining raspberry liqueur in a wide frying pan over medium heat. Set the turkey into the pan, cover, and poach, 3 to 4 minutes for cooked meat, 5 to 7 minutes for uncooked.

4 Arrange the turkey on warm serving plates. Spoon the glaze over them and serve.

Good Pans = Time Saved

The kind of cooking equipment you use will greatly influence the speed at which your recipes will cook. Use cookware with excellent heat-distribution properties—such as cast-aluminum or copper—and you will find the cooking process much more efficient.

Turkey Picadillo

I've seen a dozen dishes with the name *picadillo*, each with different preparations and ingredients. Technically, a *picadillo* should probably be called a stew, one that usually has olives and either raisins or currants in it. Loosely translated from the Spanish, it means "hash," but it's a much more elegant dish than that word implies.

In planning one of my traditional Thanksgiving Day "What Are You Gonna Do with All That Turkey?" specials on QVC, I thought I might try a quick-cooking skillet *picadillo*, one that could make use of cooked turkey. This version worked out perfectly.

1 tablespoon olive oil
1 ½ pounds turkey meat, cut into chunks (cooked or uncooked)
1 large onion, chopped
2 garlic cloves, minced
1 medium green pepper, seeded and chopped
1 15-ounce can tomato sauce
1 cup dry white wine
1 jalapeño pepper, thinly sliced
1 ½ teaspoons dried oregano
1 teaspoon dried thyme
1 ½ pounds small red-skinned potatoes, cut into ⅛-inch slices
½ cup thinly sliced pimiento-stuffed olives
½ cup raisins or currants
1 cup shelled peas
¼ cup slivered almonds

1 Heat the oil in a 12- or 14-inch skillet over medium heat. Add the turkey and cook, turning often so meat browns evenly. This will take very little time if you are using cooked turkey. Add the onion, garlic, and green pepper. Cook until the onion is wilted, stirring occasionally, about 1 to 2 minutes.

2 Add the tomato sauce, wine, jalapeño, oregano, and thyme; cook and stir until sauce comes to a vigorous simmer. Simmer uncovered for 4 to 5 minutes.

3 In a medium saucepan, place the potatoes in about ½-inch-deep slightly salted water. Bring to a boil and cook until potatoes can be easily pierced with a fork, about 5 minutes. Add the olives, raisins, and peas, and simmer another 2 minutes.

4 Serve the turkey with its sauce in the center of a warmed plate. Surround with the potato mixture, and sprinkle with the slivered almonds. Serve hot.

Turkey Scallopine

Veal Scallopine is a marvelously simple dish to prepare, but if you're watching your fat intake, it won't fit into the program. But exchange the veal for turkey, and you can enjoy this classic lemon-accented dish without feeling guilty. Another nice way to take care of some leftover turkey.

1 pound sliced turkey breast (if using cooked, slice it ⅛ to ¼ inch thick; if using fresh, slice ¼ inch thick and pound to ⅛ inch between 2 sheets of waxed paper)
2 tablespoons flour
1 tablespoon oil
½ cup lemon juice
2 tablespoons drained capers
1 lemon, thinly sliced
Hot cooked rice

1 Dust the turkey with flour and shake off any excess. Heat the oil in a 12-inch skillet over medium-high heat. Add the turkey and cook, turning once, until golden on both sides, about 4 to 5 minutes (or less if the turkey is precooked). Transfer to a warm platter and keep warm.

2 To any remaining pan juices add the lemon juice and the capers. Bring to a boil and cook, stirring, until thickened slightly.

3 Place the turkey slices over hot cooked rice on individual serving plates. Spoon the lemon-caper sauce over the turkey and serve immediately.

Beef with a Garlic-Sherry Sauce

It's hard to beat the flavor of a good piece of beef, though the mix of garlic and sherry in this sauce is a commendable enhancement. It's a fast cook, in either a wok or large skillet.

¼ cup olive oil
2 pounds boneless top
   round steak, cut into
   ¾-inch cubes
1 medium onion,
   chopped
2 garlic cloves, finely
   minced
2 tablespoons flour
1 cup beef broth
¾ cup dry sherry
½ teaspoon salt
¼ teaspoon pepper
Hot cooked wild rice
   (if desired)
Finely chopped parsley

1 Heat the oil in a wok or large skillet until hot. Add the beef and cook, turning constantly, until brown on all sides, about 2 to 3 minutes. Remove with a slotted spoon and keep warm.

2 In the remaining juices, sauté the onion and garlic until wilted, about 1 to 2 minutes. Remove the pan from the heat and carefully blend in the flour. When smooth, add the broth, sherry, salt, and pepper. Return the beef to the pan, and return the pan to medium-high heat.

3 Heat to boiling, stirring constantly, then reduce the heat to produce a gentle simmer. Simmer only as long as it takes to bring the beef to the desired level of doneness (rare, medium, etc.). Sauce should be thickened by that time.

4 Serve over wild rice, if desired, and sprinkle with the parsley before serving.

Rinderrouladen
German Stuffed Beef Rolls

Makes 4 to 6 servings

On my yearly trips to Germany for QVC, there are two dishes I seek out immediately. One is Kartoffelsuppe, or German potato soup (see Soups, Stews, and Chilis). The other is Rinderrouladen. Preparation of these beef rolls differs in various regions of Germany. Some cooks stuff them with cabbage, others with almost nothing. This version was a particularly interesting one, and probably closer to the traditional. I enjoyed it in a small family-run restaurant near the town of Hermle.

I realize this recipe takes a bit longer to complete than the others in this book, but I decided to add it anyway. It's one of my favorites, and too good not to include.

2 pounds boneless beef round steak, about ½ inch thick
Salt and pepper to taste
2 tablespoons yellow mustard
3 slices lean bacon, halved
1 medium onion, chopped
¼ cup coarsely chopped fresh parsley
3 dill pickles, halved
2 tablespoons vegetable oil
1¼ cups water
½ teaspoon salt
¼ teaspoon pepper
2 tablespoons cold water
1 tablespoon flour

1 Place the beef between 2 sheets of waxed paper, and using a wooden mallet, pound to a thickness of about ¼ inch. Cut pieces that measure approximately 7 inches long by 4 inches wide. Lightly sprinkle salt and pepper on each. Then spread a teaspoon of mustard on each piece. Place a half strip of bacon down the center of the beef, then sprinkle with a bit of chopped onion and parsley.

2 Place half a pickle on the narrowest end of the beef section, and roll it up in the beef. Secure it with toothpicks and set aside until all rolls are made.

3 Heat the oil in a skillet over medium heat until hot. Place the rolls in the skillet, add the water, and sprinkle the rolls with the ½ teaspoon salt and ¼ teaspoon pepper. Heat to boiling, then reduce the heat and simmer, covered, for about 1 hour.

4 Remove the Rinderrouladen to a warm platter and keep warm. Add enough water to the liquid in the skillet to make approximately 1 cup. In a small bowl, mix the cold water with the flour, and blend until smooth. Add it to the cooking liquid, then heat to boiling, stirring constantly, until the gravy has thickened. Pour over the Rinderrouladen and serve.

Beef in Pepper Sauce

Makes 4 servings

This quick-cooking Ethiopian dish is marked by the peppery flavor Ethiopians love. They call it *zilzil alecha* and eat it wrapped in a thin bread called *buddeena.* I came across the recipe in *Betty Crocker's New International Cookbook,* but have cut the amounts down a little and added one or two things to heat it up a bit more. I have also prepared the dish with chicken instead of beef, and have served it stuffed into pita breads.

1½ pounds boneless beef sirloin, trimmed of fat and cut into 1½-inch-long strips

2 red bell peppers, 1 coarsely chopped and 1 cut into ½-inch strips

1 jalapeño pepper, seeded and chopped

2 garlic cloves, halved

¼ cup dry white wine

¾ tablespoon minced fresh ginger

1 teaspoon salt

½ teaspoon pepper

½ teaspoon ground turmeric

¼ teaspoon ground cardamom

2 to 3 drops hot sauce, like Tabasco

1 tablespoon butter or margarine

1 tablespoon oil

1 medium onion, chopped

Hot cooked rice or pita breads (as you desire)

1 Place the chopped red pepper, jalapeño, garlic, wine, ginger, salt, pepper, turmeric, cardamom, and Tabasco in a blender on medium-high speed until smoothly blended.

2 Heat the butter or margarine and the oil in a 12-inch skillet over medium-high heat until hot. Add the beef and cook until most of the liquid has been rendered and meat is browned on all sides, about 3 to 4 minutes. Remove the beef and keep warm.

3 Add the onion and red pepper strips to the skillet and cook until wilted, about 3 minutes. Return the beef to the skillet and add the blender mixture. Heat to boiling, then reduce the heat and simmer uncovered until the beef is hot and the sauce is slightly thickened. Serve over rice or stuffed into pitas, with rice on the side.

Strip It

Cutting beef—or chicken, veal, and pork, for that matter—into strips cuts the cooking time greatly. Whenever looking over a recipe, consider whether stripping the meat will gain time without sacrificing the overall look of the dish. If it won't, cut the meat into strips and save the time.

"In-and-Out" Skillet Beef

Makes 4 servings

This is a recipe that my mother used to make in one of those old electric skillets. She would whip it up on those nights when I had Boy Scouts and my sister had ballet lessons, and we had to get out of the house in a hurry. My father was the one who added the sherry in later years (he actually started with bourbon, but toned it down). Electric skillets are relics now, but I've had no trouble duplicating my mother's "In-and-Out" beef dinner in a large cast-iron skillet or its aluminum, nonstick counterpart.

1 In a large skillet over medium heat, warm the roast beef. Separate the slices, and "drape" them around the pan. When warm, add the gravy, Worcestershire sauce, and salt. Cook and stir, blending the ingredients well and coating as much of the roast beef as possible.

1 pound rare roast beef, sliced deli style, then cut into strips
1 14¾-ounce can beef gravy
1 or 2 dashes Worcestershire sauce
1 teaspoon salt
⅓ cup sherry
1 pound fresh tomatoes, chopped
1 large onion, thinly sliced
6 to 8 ounces fresh mushrooms, sliced
1 16-ounce can peas and carrots, drained

2 Add the sherry and cook for 1 to 2 minutes. Then add the tomatoes, onion, mushrooms, and peas and carrots. Stir to blend all ingredients, then cover and simmer for about 5 minutes, or until vegetables are hot. Serve hot with garlic bread.

Pork Tenderloins
with Orange-Pepper Sauce

Makes 3 to 4 servings

12 ounces pork
    tenderloin, trimmed
    of fat
3 tablespoons flour
2 tablespoons margarine
    or butter
¼ cup chopped shallots
¾ teaspoon coarsely
    ground black pepper
⅓ cup dry white wine
1 tablespoon shredded
    orange peel
⅔ cup orange juice

If there's a simpler-to-prepare, more impressive-to-serve pork dish than this, I'd like to have it. The mix of orange and pork is exquisite.

1 Prepare the pork by cutting into ½-inch slices, then pounding between 2 sheets of waxed paper until about ¼ inch thick. Dust lightly with the flour.

2 In a wide skillet, melt the margarine over medium-high heat. Add the pork, turning once, until browned on both sides. Do this step in stages if pan isn't large enough to handle all the pork at once. When pork is browned on the outside, it should be thoroughly cooked through. Remove to a warmed serving platter, and keep warm in a 200 degree oven.

3 To the drippings in the pan add the shallots and pepper. Cook, stirring occasionally, until the shallots wilt, then add the wine, orange peel, and orange juice. Bring to a boil, stirring frequently. Cook until reduced to ½ cup or so. Pour the sauce over the pork and serve.

Pork with Red Peppers

This Spanish recipe was originally created by the Sunset kitchens as a casserole-style stew, using large cuts of pork and requiring about an hour to prepare. That would have made it impossible to present on *In the Kitchen with Bob*, of course, so I set about transforming a casserole into a quick skillet dish. A little nip here, a little tuck there, and I had the same great look and taste in a fraction of the time.

WINE MARINADE
1 ½ cups dry white wine
2 bay leaves
½ teaspoon salt
1 teaspoon paprika
3 garlic cloves, minced

1 ½ pounds boneless pork, trimmed of fat
2 teaspoons olive oil
2 medium onions, thinly sliced
2 medium tomatoes, peeled and chopped
⅛ teaspoon crushed dried hot red chili peppers
2 medium red bell peppers, seeded and cut into thin strips about ¼ inch wide or less
¼ cup chopped fresh cilantro

1 Prepare the marinade and set aside.

2 Cut the pork into thin strips about ⅜ inch wide by 2 or 3 inches long. Add the pork to the marinade, cover, and refrigerate for 6 to 8 hours, or overnight. When ready to prepare the dish, lift the pork from the marinade container, drain, and save the marinade.

3 In a wide, 4- or 5-quart pot, combine the pork, oil, and onions over high heat. Cook, stirring constantly, until onions are wilted and pork is no longer pink, about 3 to 4 minutes. Add ½ cup of the marinade and bring to a boil. Reduce heat to obtain a vigorous simmer. Add the tomatoes, dried chilies, and remaining marinade. Loosen any browned bits and stir them into the liquid.

4 Reduce the heat to low, and simmer 3 to 5 minutes, or until pork is done. Add the red peppers and cilantro, and cook only until the peppers are crisp-tender, about 3 minutes. Ladle into wide bowls and serve hot.

Pork, Rice, and Cabbage Rolls

Makes 4 servings

Here's a classic German recipe from the Bowersox family files. My father said he remembered his grandfather making them, so it's been with us for at least four generations. I've added my generation's touches with the spices, which weren't mentioned in the recipe handed down to me. They're quick and easy to make, and fun for the kids to get involved with as well. The prep can be done in minutes. Then you let the oven take over to complete the job.

¾ **pound ground pork**
½ **cup white rice**
1 ½ **teaspoons salt**
¼ **teaspoon pepper**
¼ **teaspoon dried sage**
¼ **teaspoon dried marjoram**
8 **cabbage leaves**
1 **small onion, minced**
1 **tablespoon vegetable oil**
1 **10¾-ounce condensed can tomato soup**
¾ **cup water**

1 Preheat the oven to 375 degrees.

2 In a bowl, combine the pork, rice, salt, pepper, sage, and marjoram. Set aside.

3 Cook the cabbage leaves in boiling salted water until limp. Remove carefully and lay out on paper towels to drain. Fill the wide end of each leaf with about ⅓ cup of the meat mixture, then roll the leaf about one-third of the way down. Fold in the two sides to form a sort of package, then roll the rest of the way. Place the rolled cabbage leaves in a baking dish, seam side down. Set aside momentarily.

4 Meanwhile, cook the onion in the oil in a saucepan over high heat for 3 to 4 minutes. Add the soup and water, mix well, and when hot, pour over the cabbage rolls. Cover and bake for about 1½ hours. Serve with sauce ladled over the rolls.

Pork and Green Onion Stir-Fry

Makes 2 servings

½ pound boneless
  pork loin
1 tablespoon cornstarch
1 tablespoon dry sherry
2 tablespoons vege-
  table oil
½ pound green onions,
  cut into slivers
  (including tops)
3 garlic cloves, minced
Salt and pepper to taste
Hot cooked rice

One of the things I like most about oriental cooking is its dynamics. You can have one dish that is heavily sweet, another that is on the sour side, still another that is pungent and tangy. This stir-fry is *very* subtle, its lightness punctuated by the green onions and the sherry. It's also very simple to make, and would be a good first go for anyone just starting out with a wok. This would also be a good recipe to try in crepes.

1 On a hard surface or cutting board, cut the pork across the grain into thin slices. Then cut the slices lengthwise into matchstick strips.

2 In a small bowl, combine the cornstarch and the sherry. Add the pork to the bowl, stirring to coat evenly. If you'd like a heavier flavor, marinate at least an hour, but you can cook immediately, if you'd prefer.

3 Bring a wok to high heat, and when hot, add the oil. When oil is hot, add the pork mixture and stir-fry 2 to 3 minutes. Add the green onions and garlic and continue to cook, stirring constantly, for another 2 to 3 minutes. Season with the salt and pepper. Serve over hot rice, or in a bowl by itself with the rice on the side.

Freeze a Few Crepes

On an afternoon when you have a little extra time, make a small plateful of crepes and freeze them for later use. They freeze well, and thaw quickly, and are a great way to put together a fast, different dish. I suggest putting waxed paper between crepes as you make them—they'll peel off smoothly once thawed.

Garlic Pork Chops
with Balsamic Vinegar

Makes 6 servings

I include this recipe exactly as I found it in the *Low Fat Cookbook.* It is, quite simply, absolutely delicious. For a program, I was in search of dishes that had low fat and low cholesterol as their focus, and was fortunate to have the cookbook recommended to me. Being German, I grew up loving pork chops. Being me, I couldn't resist the combination of garlic, one of my true addictions, and balsamic vinegar, the dark, rich flavor of which I am fast growing to love.

6 center-cut pork chops (about 2 pounds), trimmed of fat
Freshly ground pepper
Vegetable oil
1 head of garlic, separated into peeled cloves
1 12-ounce package eggless noodles
¼ cup sweet vermouth
1 tablespoon Dijon mustard
⅓ cup balsamic vinegar
Salt to taste

1 After trimming the chops of all fat, sprinkle them generously with the pepper.

2 Wipe a wide frying pan or skillet with oil, and cook the chops over medium-high heat until browned on one side. Turn them over, and arrange the garlic cloves around and among them. Continue to cook until chops are browned on the second side, about 3 to 4 minutes total.

3 Cook the noodles until tender to the bite, in slightly salted water.

4 While noodles are cooking, mix the vermouth and mustard in a small bowl, then pour over the browned chops. Cook until the chops are just barely pink in the center, about 4 to 5 minutes more, depending on thickness.

5 Drain the noodles and transfer to a warmed platter. Arrange the chops over the noodles and keep warm.

6 Add the vinegar to the juices in the pan. Increase the heat and stir to scrape up any browned bits on the bottom of the pan. Bring to a boil and reduce the liquid quickly to about ½ cup. Season the sauce with salt, and then spoon over each chop. Serve hot.

Lamb Curry

Makes 4 servings

CURRY POWDER
1 teaspoon each ground
    coriander, ground
    turmeric, ground black
    pepper
1 ¼ teaspoons ground
    cumin
¾ teaspoon ground
    poppy seeds
¾ teaspoon ground
    cardamom
¼ teaspoon ground
    mustard seeds
¼ teaspoon ground
    ginger
1 teaspoon ground
    chilies or chili powder
½ teaspoon ground
    cinnamon

1 pound boneless lamb
    loin, trimmed of fat
1 tablespoon vege-
    table oil
1 large onion, thinly
    sliced
2 garlic cloves, minced
1 medium carrot, thinly
    sliced into rounds
1 small green apple,
    peeled, cored, and
    chopped
1 small green bell
    pepper, seeded and
    chopped
1 10¾-ounce can beef
    broth
Salt to taste
Cayenne pepper to taste
Hot cooked rice

Curries are often thought of strictly as very hot and spicy, but in actuality they can range from hot and spicy to very mild. We usually just reach for the jar of curry powder on the supermarket shelf when a recipe calls for it, but curries are so much more vibrant if you make the powder yourself. It's simply a matter of blending the right spices.

This recipe does just that—it asks you to make the curry yourself. It's actually quite simple to do, as the ingredients are just mixed together, then added. The Lamb Curry will cook up quickly, too, and surprise you with it's tasty, nonfiery flavors.

1 Prepare the curry powder by combining all ingredients in a small bowl and blending. Set aside 1 tablespoon for use in recipe, saving any excess for future use.

2 Cut the lamb into strips about ¼ inch wide. Heat the oil in a wide frying pan over medium-high heat. Add the lamb and cook quickly, turning frequently to brown on all sides. Remove and keep warm.

3 To the juices left in the pan add the onion and curry powder, and stir until the onion wilts. Stir in the garlic, carrot, apple, green pepper, and broth. Boil gently to reduce and thicken the liquid slightly and cook until the carrots are tender to pierce, about 5 minutes. Return the lamb and cook just long enough to heat through. Season with salt and cayenne (the more you add, the more bite the dish will have). Serve with or over rice.

Side Dishes and Vegetables

"Vegetable" is derived from the Middle Latin verb, "uegere," which means to animate or enliven, to invigorate or arouse.

—Paraphrased from the
Dictionary of Word and
Phrase Origins
by William and Mary Morris

Side dishes are odd creatures. With some main dishes, they're a welcome and necessary character in the play—like a strand of pearls with an elegant dress, the side dish and entree complement each other. With other dishes, however, they can appear as an unwelcome guest—out of place. Making sure you have the former on your plate requires a bit of thought, and is always one of my most considered decisions.

The side dish must always complement—in color, texture, and flavor—the entree it is served with. It mustn't compete, though it should have the ability to distinctively stand on its own, perhaps as a main dish itself, such as the Succotash with Noodles, Tomato Pie, or Vegetable Kabobs included here.

The Herbed Zucchini, marvelously infused with its mix of Italian seasonings, is great with chicken or pasta (in fact, you might try it as a pasta sauce by dicing the zucchini a bit finer). Goebel's Special Sauerkraut is the finest I've ever tasted, and is a perfect choice for pork. Try my

Kitchen Sink Potatoes one morning as a side for scrambled eggs or an omelet, and the Potatoes Provençale, with their light touch of thyme and garlic, are wonderful with a simple beef dish, or poached fish. My mother's Sweet Potato Puffs, with their sweet surprise inside, have always been a perfect complement to turkey, as has the Celery and Carrots in a Cream Sauce.

My suggestion is to start with color first. If your main dish is a light one, such as chicken or white-fleshed fish, pick a side with some vibrant color or a mix of colors (the Quick Pepper Sauté) to complement it. Then consider how the flavors will work with one another. If your main dish is heavily spiced, a lighter side dish, perhaps with a touch of sweetness, like the Green Beans with Bermuda Onions, or Honey-Glazed Carrots, would be a good choice. Whatever your plans, I'm sure you'll find at least one side dish here that will work for you.

Herbed Zucchini

Makes 4 servings

Zucchini alone is not always an impressive addition to a meal. But add an arsenal of herbs and a simple side dish becomes an extraordinary one. At home, we often use this combination of herbs for yellow squash or potatoes as well. It cooks quickly, so prepare just before serving.

3 tablespoons olive oil
1 or 2 medium to large zucchini, sliced into ⅛-inch-thick rounds
1 ½ tablespoons butter or margarine
1 teaspoon chopped garlic
1 tablespoon finely chopped dried tarragon
1 tablespoon finely chopped dried basil
½ tablespoon finely chopped dried chives
1 tablespoon finely chopped fresh parsley
Salt and pepper to taste

1 Heat the olive oil in a medium skillet over medium-high heat. When very hot, add the zucchini and cook for 2 to 3 minutes. Turn the vegetable at least once.

2 Drain the oil from the pan, and add the butter or margarine and all herbs, plus salt and pepper. Reduce heat and turn vegetables several times to ensure even coating with the herbs. Serve hot.

Green Beans with Bermuda Onions

Makes 4 to 6 servings

This is one of my favorite side dishes. It takes only minutes to prepare, and has a beautiful mix of colors if not overcooked. Use the freshest green beans you can, as they have a brightness to their flavor that is a perfect match for the tangy sweetness of the Bermuda onion.

1 pound green beans
2 tablespoons butter or margarine
1 medium Bermuda onion, chopped
Salt and pepper to taste

1 Cut the ends of the beans with a diagonal cut, then cook in lightly salted boiling water for 5 minutes (they should be bright green and crisp).

2 While the beans are cooking, melt the butter or margarine in a high-sided frying pan or large saucepan over medium-high heat. Add the onion and sauté just until it begins to look translucent.

3 Drain the beans thoroughly and place in a serving bowl. Immediately pour the onion over the beans, season with salt and pepper, and toss until blended. Serve hot.

Don't Overcook

Cook your vegetables only until they are crisp-tender. They will be ready faster, be more flavorful, and retain more of their natural color and nutritional value.

Sweet-and-Sour Carrots

Makes 6 to 8 servings

I have always loved that unique mix of flavors that Asian dishes achieve as "sweet and sour." Here's a quickly prepared side dish version for carrots, which lend themselves well to the peculiar blend of tastes.

1 pound carrots, sliced
  into ⅛-inch rounds
1 green bell pepper,
  seeded and chopped
1 bunch green onions,
  chopped (including
  tops)
1 10¾-ounce can
  condensed tomato soup
½ cup cider vinegar
½ cup vegetable oil
1 cup sugar
1 tablespoon dry
  mustard
Salt and pepper to taste

1 Cook the carrots in boiling water until crisp-tender, about 3 to 5 minutes, and set aside.

2 In a saucepan over high heat, place all other ingredients and bring to a boil. As soon as it boils, pour over the carrots and serve.

Goebel's Special Sauerkraut

Makes 4 to 6 servings

I travel to Germany once a year for QVC to visit a number of manufacturers and artists whose products we feature throughout the year. In 1992, we visited the M. I. Hummel factory in Rodenthal, Germany, where the world-famous figurines are handcrafted. After our visit, we were cordially invited to a special lunch with the president and his top aides in their private dining room.

We were served a traditional knockwurst and sauerkraut lunch. While the knockwurst was typical, the sauerkraut was remarkable. In fact, it was absolutely the best I had ever had. It was creamy and rich, but without the hard edge that sauerkraut can have. I politely begged for the recipe, and was very graciously taken back to the kitchen, where the Goebel chef shared this recipe.

**2 pounds sauerkraut
(2 16-ounce cans)
½ cup sugar
1 cup dark German beer
2 bay leaves**

Combine all the ingredients in a slow cooker and cook until the sauerkraut achieves a very creamy texture. Add more beer if it seems to be drying out. Remove bay leaves. Serve hot.

Snowpeas with a Cool Mint Sauce

Makes 4 to 6 servings

Originally created by the Sunset kitchens as an hor d'oeuvre dip, I thought this might make a great side dish to an oriental entree. I adapted the recipe and was pleasantly rewarded with a refreshing addition to my meal.

1 pound snowpeas
¼ cup sour cream, at room temperature
¼ cup mayonnaise, at room temperature
3 tablespoons chopped fresh mint leaves
Fresh mint sprigs (as garnish)

1 In a wide skillet, cook the snowpeas in lightly salted water until crisp-tender, about 3 minutes. Don't overcook them. They should be hot, bright green, and snap when you bend them.

2 While beans are cooking, place the sour cream, mayonnaise, and chopped mint in a food processor or blender and whirl until blended thoroughly.

3 Arrange the beans, fan-style, on the individual, warmed serving plates and top immediately with a tablespoon of the cool mint sauce. Serve immediately.

A Little Salt = Quicker Boil

Add a little salt to the water in your pot, and it will come to a boil faster.

Brussels Sprouts in a Mustard Glaze

Makes 4 servings

1 ½ pounds Brussels sprouts

3 tablespoons firmly packed brown sugar

2 tablespoons cider vinegar

1 tablespoon Dijon mustard

2 teaspoons margarine or butter

Salt to taste

This is a terrific accompaniment to pork, whether it be chops or roast. You'll have them on the table in under ten minutes, and if a little of the glaze rubs off on the pork, so much the better. Though there are any number of glaze recipes, I found this version for sprouts in the *Low Fat Cookbook.*

 Clean the Brussels sprouts by cutting off the bottom $\frac{1}{16}$ inch of stem and discarding the loose outer leaves. Rinse and drain, then steam for 8 to 10 minutes.

2 When sprouts are nearly done (about 5 minutes into their cooking cycle), combine the brown sugar, vinegar, mustard, margarine, and salt in a wide frying pan over medium-high heat. When mixture bubbles, stir in the sprouts, and turn them to coat them evenly. Serve immediately.

Potatoes Provençale

Makes 6 to 8 servings

The simple touch of the French peasants can be tasted in this dish. People in the Provence region of France love to use garlic and herbs. In this case the touch is a subtle one, and a nice complement to chicken or fish.

6 small to medium baking potatoes, sliced 1/16 inch thick

Salt and pepper to taste

2 tablespoons virgin olive oil

1 large onion, finely chopped

2 tablespoons unsalted butter or margarine

2 garlic cloves, minced

3/4 teaspoon chopped fresh thyme or 1/8 teaspoon dried

1 Rinse potato slices in cool water, sprinkle with salt and pepper, then dry them on paper towels.

2 In a wide skillet or frying pan, sauté the onion in the butter over medium-high heat. Add the garlic and thyme. Add the potatoes and cook, turning frequently until golden brown, about 5 to 7 minutes. Serve hot.

Bob's Kitchen Sink Potatoes

Makes 4 to 6 servings

3 tablespoons oil
1 teaspoon salt
4 medium potatoes, peeled and diced into ⅜-inch cubes
2 garlic cloves, minced
¼ cup beef broth
½ teaspoon Worcestershire sauce
½ cup chopped onion
½ cup chopped green bell pepper
½ cup chopped and drained pimientos
¼ cup chopped celery

This side dish came about by looking through the refrigerator, seeing what was there, and putting it all together. I enjoy the adventure of the process because, more often than not, I create a dish I'll want to make again and again because it came out so well. This is one of those dishes. I've found that it is also excellent with eggs for a breakfast or brunch.

1 Heat the oil in a large skillet over high heat until hot. Add the potatoes, garlic, and salt and sauté for 3 to 4 minutes, turning frequently.

2 Combine the broth with the Worcestershire sauce, and pour over the potatoes. Bring to a boil. Add the vegetables, stir to blend, cover, and steam for another 5 to 6 minutes.

3 When broth is absorbed and vegetables are crisp-tender, serve immediately.

Plan for Quick Needs

Keep a can or two of French-cut green beans handy, along with a bag of slivered almonds, or a Bermuda onion or two. You'll always have a stylish side dish only minutes away.

Succotash with Noodles

Makes 4 to 6 servings

I grew up with succotash as a staple in my mother's arsenal. By the time I was off to college, I had about had my fill, and can safely say I didn't try succotash again for over twenty-five years. But thanks to Richard Simmons, the health and exercise celebrity, I was re-introduced to its wonderful mixture of textures and flavors.

Richard has appeared on QVC many times with his cookbook, and I noticed that many of his recipes for the ordinary are enhanced by combining a few things that you wouldn't expect to find together. He often adds noodles or meat to a vegetable side dish, for instance. This quick side dish is a distilled mix of two or three others tossed together à la Richard Simmons. It takes little time to prepare, and can be easily expanded into a top-of-the-stove casserole if a one-dish meal is desired.

½ pound spicy sausage meat, loosely crumbled
2 large shallots, chopped
½ green bell pepper, seeded and chopped
1 pound tomatoes, chopped
1 10-ounce package frozen succotash, thawed
½ teaspoon salt
¼ teaspoon pepper
½ teaspoon dried oregano
1 8-ounce package flat noodles, cooked and drained
½ cup grated cheese (sharp cheddar or Parmesan)

1 In a large skillet, cook the sausage meat over medium-high heat until no longer pink, about 4 minutes. Drain any rendered fat. Add the shallots and pepper and continue to cook until vegetables are crisp-tender, about 3 to 4 minutes.

2 Add the tomatoes, succotash, salt, pepper, and oregano. Cover and steam until the lima beans can be pierced with a fork.

3 Add the noodles, then stir in the cheese and toss the entire dish to mix noodles and cheese throughout the dish. Serve hot.

Harvard Beets

Makes 4 servings

Here's a classic, often known as sweet-and-sour beets. There are as many variations of Harvard Beets as there are cooks who like to experiment with recipes, but this is the starting point for them all.

½ cup sugar
1 tablespoon cornstarch
½ teaspoon salt
½ cup cider vinegar
2 tablespoons butter or margarine
6 medium beets, cooked and sliced in ¼-inch rounds

1 In a large saucepan over high heat, combine the sugar, cornstarch, salt, and vinegar. Mix well and bring to a boil, stirring constantly. Boil for 5 minutes.

2 Reduce the heat and add the butter. When melted, add the beets and stir to coat evenly. Serve beets with sauce over them.

Quick Pepper Sauté

Makes 3 to 4 servings

This side dish grew out of my need for exceptional color on a plate. The vibrant green, yellow, and red peppers provided that color, and the mix of garlic and shallot was a perfect addition to the fresh, sweet flavors of the peppers. This is marvelous in conjunction with a poached or sautéed fish, and is also excellent with veal.

1 green bell pepper
1 red bell pepper
1 yellow bell pepper
2 tablespoons butter or margarine
1 large shallot, finely chopped
2 garlic cloves, minced

1 Clean and seed the peppers. Cut them down their length into ⅛- to ¼-inch-wide strips.

2 Melt the butter or margarine in a wide skillet or frying pan over medium-high heat. Add the shallot and garlic, and cook until wilted. Add the peppers. Toss and sauté briefly, only long enough to warm the peppers. Do not overcook them; you want them crisp-tender, not mushy. Serve hot.

Honey-Glazed Carrots

Makes 4 to 6 servings

Glazing is usually done by heating a mixture of butter and the rendered natural liquid of a vegetable until it forms the glaze. It usually adds a distinct sweetness to the vegetables, and therefore to your plate as a whole. This version uses the honey to add the sweetness, thereby eliminating the cholesterol the butter would have added. The glaze is just as effective and enjoyable.

12 medium carrots, sliced into ⅛-inch rounds
⅓ cup honey
2 tablespoons vegetable oil
1 teaspoon lemon juice
½ teaspoon salt

1 In a large saucepan, bring about 1 inch of lightly salted water to a boil. Add the carrots, and cook until crisp-tender, about 5 minutes.

2 In another saucepan, combine the remaining ingredients and cook until they reach a thick, bubbling simmer.

3 Drain the carrots thoroughly and add to the sauce. Cook over low heat, stirring frequently, until carrots are glazed, about 4 to 5 minutes. Serve hot.

Spenser's Green Apple, Onion, and Carrots

Makes 3 to 4 servings

One of my favorite ways to relax is to settle in with one of Robert B. Parker's Spenser novels. Not only are they superior examples of some of the tightest writing in fiction, but Parker's fictional private detective, Spenser, is a great cook. Parker usually gives us at least one interesting recipe in each novel. (There are twenty-three books at last count.) I tried this one the day I read it, and have used it a dozen times since. It's particularly good with pork.

2 or 3 garlic cloves, finely chopped

1 medium Bermuda onion, sliced into ⅛-inch rings

2 tablespoons butter or margarine

1 cup apple cider

2 medium carrots, julienned 2 inches long by ¼-inch thick

2 Granny Smith apples, sliced into ⅛-inch wedges

1 In a skillet over medium-high heat, sauté the garlic and onion in the butter or margarine until translucent.

2 Add ½ cup of the apple cider and the carrots and bring to a vigorous simmer. Cook for 5 minutes. Add the apples and simmer for about 1 minute, then add the rest of the cider. Simmer for another 5 minutes, then serve hot.

Herbed Tomatoes Languedocienne

The Languedoc region of France borders the Provence region in southern France, and, as in Provence, people there use a lot of fruits and vegetables, garlic, and herbs in their cooking. This preparation of herbed tomatoes is one you might find on any resident's table for lunch or dinner.

4 large, ripe tomatoes
Salt
4 slices white bread, crusts removed
2 tablespoons olive oil
2 garlic cloves, minced
1 tablespoon finely chopped fresh parsley
2 teaspoons chopped, dried thyme
1 teaspoon chopped, dried basil
½ teaspoon salt
¼ teaspoon pepper

1 About 1½ hours before you need to prepare the dish, cut the tomatoes in half and sprinkle each half with salt. Place them upside down in a strainer or colander to drain.

2 When ready to prepare the dish, preheat the oven to 350 degrees. Rinse the tomatoes and with a teaspoon, carefully scoop out most of the pulp and any remaining juice. Do not damage the walls of the tomatoes or make them too thin. Set the halves in a long casserole or baking dish.

3 Combine the oil and garlic, and with a small pastry brush, brush both sides of the bread with the mixture. Let it soften for 1 to 2 minutes, then chop the bread. Sprinkle the herbs, salt, and pepper over the pieces.

4 Lightly press the herbed bread pieces into the tomato halves, and sprinkle with any remaining butter and garlic mix.

5 Bake for 5 minutes, then flash under a broiler for another 2 or 3 minutes until the bread filling is browned. Serve immediately.

Vegetable Kabobs

**For each serving
(2 kabobs)**

Sometimes you can take some average vegetables and let your presentation spruce them up a bit to bring your side dish a little panache. Kabobs can do that nicely for you. The mixture of vegetables is really up to you—I'll start you with a mix here (I like the use of both white and sweet potatoes—they need to be cooked ahead of time, so this is a good way to use some leftover 'taters), but don't let this grouping be iron-clad. Experiment a bit by adding some yellow squash or zucchini, or perhaps a Brussels sprout or two.

**2 1-inch cubes of baking
potato
1 1-inch cube of sweet
potato
2 small onions, peeled
2 or 3 small, whole
mushrooms
2 1-inch squares of green
bell pepper
2 1-inch squares of red
bell pepper
1 or 2 cherry tomatoes
Melted butter or
margarine
Salt and pepper to taste
Hot cooked rice
Garlic bread (optional)**

1 Thread the vegetables onto 8-inch bamboo skewers in whatever order suits you. Leave ½ to ¾ inch on either end for handling.

2 Dip the kabobs in the melted butter, then dust with salt and pepper (or your choice of herbs). Brown under a broiler, or on a grill, turning every 1 to 2 minutes so all sides cook evenly. Serve on a bed of rice, with hot garlic bread on the side.

Marilee's
Sweet Potato Puffs

Makes 4 to 6 servings

There wasn't a Thanksgiving or Christmas dinner in my mother's house that didn't feature her famous Sweet Potato Puffs. She made them only on those two occasions, and family and neighborhood friends waited patiently all year for them.

They are as simple to make as forming a snowball, and make great fun for the kids gathered for family holidays. The surprise inside is what makes the dish—and makes you look forward to them every year.

2 18-ounce cans whole and cut sweet potatoes
Flour
Marshmallows (the large ones)
Crushed corn flakes
Dark brown sugar
Dark corn syrup

1 Preheat the oven to 350 degrees.

2 Put the sweet potatoes in a large bowl, and drain as much of the residual liquid from them as possible. Gently mash all pieces together.

3 Dust your hands with a little flour, and gently knock off any excess. Take a palmful of sweet potato in one hand, and place a marshmallow in the center of the mass. Place a second palmful of sweet potato on top of the first, surrounding the marshmallow totally. Gently form a "snowball" of sweet potato, then gently roll it in a bowl of corn flake crumbs—just enough to get some stuck around the puff.

4 Place the puffs in a baking dish. Sprinkle about 1 tablespoon of brown sugar on top of each puff, so that it covers the top in a thin layer. Drizzle 1 to 2 tablespoons of corn syrup over the brown sugar and top of each puff, so that it runs down the sides a bit.

5 Bake for about 20 minutes, or until the brown sugar has melted slightly over the top. Serve hot.

Celery and Carrots in a Cream Sauce

Makes 4 servings

4 large carrots
6 celery stalks
Salt and freshly ground pepper to taste
6 tablespoons butter or margarine
¼ teaspoon grated nutmeg
½ cup heavy cream

This is an elegant side dish, with subtle flavors and a light pastel color. It's a great match of light flavors and heavy sauce, with the nutmeg adding just the right balance.

1 Trim and scrape the carrots, then cut into ¼-inch square slices 1½ inches long. Cut the celery in the same manner. Place the carrot and celery pieces in a saucepan with just enough water to cover them and salt to taste. Bring to a boil and simmer for about 8 minutes or until the vegetables are crisp-tender.

2 In a second saucepan, heat the butter or margarine over medium heat. Drain the carrots and celery well, and add to the butter or margarine. Add salt and pepper and the nutmeg. Add the cream, stir thoroughly, and simmer for another 3 to 4 minutes or until the cream thickens slightly. Serve hot.

Tomato Pie

I include Tomato Pie in this section because it does make a nice side dish, but it might just as well be a one-dish entree—it's a fine alternative to the heaviness of quiche. Regardless of how you use it, Tomato Pie is for die-hard tomato lovers. It's my sister Maggie's recipe, and we try to make it only when tomatoes are at their peak of flavor and firmness.

1 9-inch baked pie shell
3 large tomatoes, sliced
  ½ inch thick
Salt and pepper to taste
1 tablespoon chopped
  dried basil
½ pound Swiss cheese,
  sliced
2 medium onions, sliced
  in thin rings
½ cup grated Parmesan
  cheese

1 Preheat the oven to 350 degrees.

2 Line the pie shell with half the tomato slices. Sprinkle with the salt, pepper, and basil. Layer half the Swiss cheese on top of the tomatoes, then cover with a layer of the onions. Repeat the layers, starting with the tomatoes.

3 Sprinkle the top of the pie with the Parmesan cheese, and bake until bubbly. Serve hot. If serving as a one-dish meal, serve with a green salad on the side.

Baking a Pie Shell

To bake a pie shell with nothing in it is not the trick it may seem to be. Line the pie shell with waxed paper, and fill it with rice. Bake it for 5 to 7 minutes, or until the edges start to brown slightly. Remove from the oven and discard the waxed paper and rice.

Baked Glazed Onions

I'm a major fan of baked onions. There's a sweetness in an onion that seems to come out only when it's baked. This recipe also calls for glazing the onions with a mix of honey, mustard, and vinegar. The end result is a sweet, savory side dish that will draw raves around the table.

6 to 8 medium onions, peeled
2 tablespoons butter or margarine, softened
½ cup honey
4 teaspoons Dijon mustard
2 tablespoons red wine vinegar
1 teaspoon paprika
⅛ teaspoon ground cloves
½ teaspoon salt
½ teaspoon freshly ground pepper
½ cup water

1 Preheat the oven to 350 degrees.

2 Cut the top of each onion in an X pattern about ½ inch deep. Open the "petals" slightly with your fingers.

3 In a bowl, combine the butter, honey, mustard, and vinegar and whisk until smooth. Add the paprika, cloves, salt, and pepper and mix well. Place the onions in a casserole or baking dish. Make sure they fit snugly, and will hold each other up in the dish. Pour the water around them.

4 Spoon about 2 teaspoons of the glaze over each onion, making sure some gets into the petals you opened earlier. Bake for 30 minutes, basting often with the glaze. Add more water if it gets too low in the dish; otherwise, the onions will dry out before they are cooked. Serve hot.

Mexican Cinnamon Rice

Makes 4 servings

It's been said of me that I must have been Oriental in a past life, given my love of rice. But I counter that a love of rice can offer you a pedigree in any cuisine. We find it in the cooking of just about every nationality on earth. One of my favorites comes from Mexico, and combines the sweetness of currants with the tangy mix of onion and garlic.

½ cup chopped onion
1 garlic clove, minced
2 tablespoons margarine or butter
1 cup quick-cooking long-grain rice
¼ cup currants or raisins
2¼ cups chicken broth
2 tablespoons ground cinnamon
1 teaspoon minced fresh cilantro

1 In a saucepan over medium-high heat, cook the onion and garlic in the margarine until translucent. Stir in all the remaining ingredients except the cilantro and bring to a boil, stirring occasionally. Reduce heat and simmer for 5 minutes without stirring.

2 Just before serving, fluff the rice, add the cilantro, and fluff again. Serve hot.

Microwave Ovens

Use a microwave oven for side dishes whenever you can. It makes short work of vegetables, which will give you more time for other things.

Desserts

The daintiest last, to make the end most sweet.

—**William Shakespeare, Richard II**

What a shame it is that dessert comes last in a meal, when we are fairly satiated and left with tight belts! For it is in desserts that we find some of the most pleasing concoctions one person can offer the palate of another—inventions the sight of which alone will break down the strongest of willpowers.

I will tempt you here with only a few, but I think you'll find each exquisite. I wager that the Serious Pecan Pie is the richest and chewiest you've ever had. Both the Parfait Bleu and the Quick Cool Lemon Dessert are terrific light desserts for warmer weather, and simplicity in preparation mark Alice's Rice Pudding and the No-Bake Strawberry Torte. And if you want to make a show of dessert, the authentic Bananas Foster flambé will truly impress.

One note: several of the desserts included here require some extra time baking or chilling. That's just the nature of desserts. However, they can all be prepared far in advance of their being needed, so you won't be cramped for time when you need it most.

Serious Pecan Pie

Makes a 9-inch pie

1 9-inch pie shell,
 partially baked
⅓ cup butter or
 margarine, melted
⅔ cup packed brown
 sugar
3 large eggs
1 cup dark corn syrup
1 ¼ cups broken or
 slightly chopped
 pecans
1 tablespoon rum
½ teaspoon salt

This is a "stick-to-the-roof-of-your-mouth" kind of pie, a "better-have-a-toothpick" kind of pie, a pecan lover's kind of pie. This version comes from the Bowersox family archives, developed over many years first by my father, then by my brother and me.

1 Preheat the oven to 450 degrees.

2 Bake the empty pie shell about 8 minutes (see page 143). Allow it to cool while preparing filling. Reduce oven temperature to 375 degrees.

3 In a mixing bowl, cream the butter and brown sugar. Beat in the eggs, one at a time, until smooth. Stir in the corn syrup, pecans, rum, and salt, blending thoroughly.

4 Pour mixture into the pie shell. Bake for 40 to 45 minutes, or until a knife inserted into the filling comes out clean. Serve warm with vanilla ice cream. Also good served cold, though much chewier.

Bananas Foster

Makes 6 servings

This is the famous dessert created at Brennan's Restaurant in New Orleans. Of lesser note, perhaps, it was one of the most requested desserts served at my restaurant in Delaware, The Crepe Chalet. I prepared and served Bananas Foster as the original was, flamed over vanilla ice cream. It's an impressive dessert to make tableside for your guests. Just make sure they—and you—are comfortable with flambé.

6 medium bananas
1 tablespoon lemon juice
¼ cup butter or
  margarine
½ cup firmly packed
  brown sugar
½ cup white rum
½ teaspoon ground
  cinnamon
¼ cup banana liqueur
Vanilla ice cream

1 Peel the bananas and cut in half lengthwise. Brush them lightly with the lemon juice to retard browning.

2 In a large skillet, chafing dish, or suzette pan, melt the butter. Add the brown sugar and 2 tablespoons of the rum. Cook, stirring, until the sugar has melted.

3 Add the bananas to the pan, and baste with the hot syrup. Sprinkle with the cinnamon.

4 Add the banana liqueur and the remaining rum. Cover the dish and cook for 1 minute. Remove the cover and ignite immediately with a long, fireplace match. Baste the bananas with the flaming sauce until flames are extinguished. Serve immediately over vanilla ice cream.

Walnut Cake with Chocolate-Walnut Butter Cream Icing

Makes 2 cakes

1 cup butter or margarine
2 cups sugar
3 cups sifted all-purpose flour, plus 1 tablespoon unsifted
1 tablespoon baking powder
¼ teaspoon salt
2 cups broken walnuts
4 large eggs, at room temperature
1 cup milk, at room temperature
1 teaspoon vanilla extract
½ teaspoon almond extract
12 whole large walnut halves (as garnish)

CHOCOLATE-WALNUT BUTTER CREAM ICING

4 ounces unsweetened chocolate
2 tablespoons strong coffee
4 large egg yolks
¼ teaspoon salt
½ cup sugar
1 cup butter or margarine
1 cup broken walnuts

I think this is one of the great cakes, not just because I happen to like walnuts quite a bit, but because I can't get enough of the icing. The mix of chocolate and walnut in a buttery icing is temptation incarnate to me. When I make this one, I make extra icing, so there's an extra thickness of it on the cake, and a little extra in the bowl for licking. I suggest serving the cake with a little Frangelico liqueur, or perhaps some Bailey's Irish Cream, on the side.

1 Preheat the oven to 350 degrees. Lightly butter two 9 by 5-inch loaf pans.

2 Cut the butter into cubes in a large mixing bowl. Gradually add the sugar and beat until creamy.

3 In a separate bowl, sift together the 3 cups flour, baking powder, and salt. Toss the broken walnut pieces with the unsifted tablespoon of flour and set aside.

4 Add the eggs one at a time to the cream mixture, beating well after each egg is added.

5 Combine the milk with the vanilla and almond extracts. Alternately add the flour mixture and the milk mixture to the cream mixture, beating well after each addition. Add the floured walnut pieces and continue to beat until well blended.

6 Spoon equal portions of the batter into each loaf pan. Bake for 50 minutes, or until a toothpick inserted into the cakes comes out clean. Let the pans cool, then turn out the cakes onto a rack.

7 In a double boiler, combine the chocolate and coffee for the icing and heat, stirring often, until the chocolate is melted and blended with the coffee.

8 In a mixing bowl, combine the yolks, salt, and sugar. Set this bowl in a basin or large stockpot of simmering water and beat rapidly with a wire whisk until the mixture runs from the whisk in a ribbon.

9 Add the chocolate mixture to the yolk mixture. Continue to beat over the simmering water. Gradually add the butter a little at a time. Remove the bowl from the heat and continue to beat, using a wooden spoon, until the icing thickens and becomes spreadable. Beat in the walnuts and beat until smooth and a bit lighter.

10 Spread the top of each cake with the icing, and garnish the tops with the half walnuts.

Parfait Bleu

Makes 4 servings

There's nothing quite as refreshing after a meal as a parfait to both the eye and the palate. Parfait Bleu gives you the cool refreshment without adding a lot of fat and cholesterol. It also won't take you more than two minutes to prepare for chilling.

**1 pint blueberries,
   picked of stems
2 8-ounce containers
   low-fat lemon yogurt
Fresh whipped cream**

1 In parfait glasses or tall, wide wine glasses, arrange alternate layers of the blueberries and yogurt. Make the top layer blueberries.

2 Chill for at least an hour before use. Top with a dollop of whipped cream just before serving.

Alice's Rice Pudding

Makes 6 to 8 servings

Alice Anthony was one of the greatest cooks I've ever known, though you would never have had the opportunity to taste her cooking—that is, unless you were fortunate enough to be invited to my grandfather's house for dinner. Alice was my grandparent's cook, and my sister and I grew up being loved, scolded, and fed by her.

Though her meals were extraordinary, it is her desserts I recall the most. Though I shall save most of the recipes I inherited from her for another tome, I share one of my favorites with you here—Alice's Rice Pudding. It's a fine example of what always has amazed me about Alice's cooking: so remarkably simple, but so incredibly good.

¾ **cup cooked white rice**
3 large eggs, beaten
2 cups whole milk
1 cup evaporated milk
½ **cup sugar**
⅛ **teaspoon salt**
1 ¼ **teaspoons vanilla extract**
Ground cinnamon

1 Preheat the oven to 350 degrees.

2 Mix all ingredients except cinnamon in a large bowl until blended. Pour into an oblong baking dish, and sprinkle generously with cinnamon.

3 Bake for 35 minutes. Serve hot or cold. (See what I mean about simple? Wait till you taste it!)

Individual Fruit Cheesecakes

Makes 18 to 22 pieces

These little beauties can be made far in advance of any party and frozen. They are particularly good for this era of participatory dining, where each guest is allowed to individualize his or her portion. A lazy Susan of fruits or compotes for toppings, and you have instant individually created fruit cheesecakes.

3 8-ounce packages cream cheese
1⅓ cups sugar
5 large eggs
1½ teaspoons vanilla extract
2 cups sour cream
Fruit for toppings: cherries, strawberries, blueberries, mandarin oranges, etc. (feel free to use pie fillings, with syrups)

1 Preheat the oven to 300 degrees.

2 Cream the cream cheese and 1 cup sugar until light and fluffy. This can be done by hand or mixer. Beat in the eggs and 1 teaspoon vanilla.

3 Spoon the mixture into individual muffin tins, filling each muffin cup about two-thirds full. If not using a nonstick muffin tin, use paper liners.

4 Bake for 40 minutes, then remove from the heat and cool. The cakes will tend to shrink into the muffin cups. This is normal.

5 Combine the sour cream with the remaining ⅓ cup sugar and ½ teaspoon vanilla, and top each cake with the mixture. Return to the oven for 5 minutes. Cool, freeze, or serve. Remove any paper liners before presentation.

California Surprise

This is almost as much fun to make as it is to eat. You build the cake in layers, adding each in succession. Though I promised efficiency in this cookbook, I must tell you that this one will take you a little extra time. But it will be worth it. Each layer is something new, and as you eat your way through a piece of this cake, you will understand its name.

½ cup soft margarine
1 cup all-purpose flour
½ cup finely chopped
   pecans
1 8-ounce package
   cream cheese, very soft
1 cup confectioners'
   sugar
1 cup Cool Whip
2 3-ounce packages
   instant vanilla pudding
3 cups milk
3 medium bananas,
   sliced into ¼-inch
   rounds
⅓ cup chopped nuts
   (peanuts, walnuts,
   cashews, or a
   mixture—your choice)

1 Preheat the oven to 350 degrees.

2 In a mixing bowl, combine the margarine, flour, and pecans. Mix with a fork or wooden spoon and press into an ungreased 9 × 13-inch baking pan. Bake for 15 minutes. Chill before continuing.

3 Mix the cream cheese, confectioners' sugar, and Cool Whip. Spread evenly on the first layer. Refrigerate until chilled.

4 In a large mixing bowl, combine the pudding mix and milk and beat with a mixer until thick. Spread on top of the second layer and refrigerate for 2 to 3 hours until firm.

5 Add the sliced bananas on top of the third layer, and top over all with a layer of Cool Whip. Sprinkle with the nuts and refrigerate until ready to serve. Cut and serve as a pan cake.

No-Bake Strawberry Torte

Makes 6 servings

4 cups sliced
  strawberries
6 tablespoons
  confectioners' sugar
1 cup brown-edged
  wafer or vanilla wafer
  crumbs
2 tablespoons butter,
  melted
1 cup whipping (heavy)
  cream
1 teaspoon vanilla
  extract
Grated sweet chocolate
  (as garnish)

This is an easy-to-make, sinful-to-eat torte that requires
no baking whatsoever. A couple of minutes of
preparation, a couple of hours of refrigeration, and you
have an elegant dessert worthy of the best five-star
restaurant. The original recipe was in the June 1986 issue
of *Ladies' Home Journal.* (It's amazing what you can find in a
dentist's waiting room!)

1 Reserve 6 strawberry slices for garnish. In a medium bowl,
combine the remaining strawberries with 4 tablespoons of
the sugar. Toss and set aside.

2 In a small bowl, combine the wafer crumbs and the butter.
Gently press them onto the bottom of a 6½-inch spring-
form pan. Drain the sliced strawberries, and arrange them
over the crumbs.

3 In a mixer bowl, or by hand, beat the cream until thickened. Add the remaining 2 tablespoons of sugar and the
vanilla. Beat until very stiff peaks form.

4 Spread two-thirds of the whipped cream over the strawberries. Sprinkle with grated chocolate. With a pastry bag fit-
ted with a medium star tube, pipe the remaining whipped
cream decoratively around the edge of the top. Refrigerate
for 2 hours. Remove pan before serving.

Quick Cool Lemon Dessert

Makes 6 to 8 servings

Want a tangy, cool, fruit dessert that makes the refrigerator do all the work? This is it. It's a perfect finish to any meal or a wonderful midday refreshment on a hot summer's day.

1 16-ounce can mandarin oranges (with juice)

1 16-ounce can pineapple bits (with juice)

1 16-ounce can fruit cocktail (with juice)

2 tablespoons lemon juice

1 3-ounce box instant lemon pudding

1 or 2 bananas, sliced

Cool Whip

1 Combine the oranges, pineapple, fruit cocktail, and lemon juice in a large bowl and toss lightly.

2 Sprinkle in the lemon pudding (do not add water or other liquid—the liquid from the fruits will handle it). Toss again and refrigerate for at least 2 hours.

3 Before serving, place the banana slices on the top. Place a dollop of Cool Whip on top of each serving.

Bibliography

Throughout this book I've mentioned a number of cookbooks in my collection that have served as inspiration or as the genesis for many of the recipe adaptations that I've used on *In the Kitchen with Bob.* Enjoy wandering through them; they are all exceptional.

Betty Crocker's New International Cookbook, edited by Diana Gulden. New York: Prentice-Hall, 1989.

Boely, Patrice. *The Joy of Seafood.* New York: Barron's, 1988.

Casas, Penelope. *Tapas, The Little Dishes of Spain.* New York: Alfred A. Knopf, 1991.

Claiborne, Craig. *The New York Times Cookbook.* New York: Times Books, 1979.

Clayton, Bernard, Jr. *The Complete Book of Soups and Stews.* New York: Simon and Schuster, 1984.

Italian Cook Book, edited by Jerry Anne Di Vecchio. Menlo Park: Sunset Publishing, 1991.

Low Cholesterol Cookbook, edited by Elizabeth L. Hogan. Menlo Park: Lane Publishing, 1990.

Low Fat Cookbook, edited by Elizabeth L. Hogan. Menlo Park: Sunset Publishing, 1991.

Quick & Easy Cook Book, edited by Elizabeth L. Hogan. Menlo Park: Sunset Publishing, 1991.

Southwest Cook Book, edited by David E. Clark. Menlo Park: Lane Publishing, 1987.

Vegetarian Cooking, edited by Janeth Johnson Nix. Menlo Park: Sunset Publishing, 1981.

Index